Related Books of Interest

Search Engine Marketing, Inc.
I, II, III, and IV LiveLessons
(Video Training)
Moran
ISBN: 978-0-13-262045-1

D1605891

Get Bold
Carter
ISBN: 978-0-13-261831-1

Making the World Work Better
Maney, Hamm, O'Brien
ISBN: 978-0-13-275510-8

Audience, Relevance, and Search
Mathewson, Donatone, Fishel
ISBN: 978-0-13-700420-1

Web 2.0 and Social Networking
for the Enterprise
Bernal
ISBN: 978-0-13-700489-8

The Social Factor
Azuza
ISBN: 978-0-13-701890-1

Praise for *Opting In*

"A must-read for anyone in business today. Ed does an incredible job at articulating the cultural shift driving social business today and the need for companies to embrace social business practices in order to thrive in today's changing digital world."
—**Jonathan Levitt**
Chief Marketing Officer, OpinionLab

"Ed gives us a highly actionable, from-the-trenches view of social business, how it works, and why it will reshape how we do business."
—**Dion Hinchcliffe**
Chief Strategy Officer, Dachis Group
Columnist for ZDNet and InformationWeek

"I have been teaching Internet Marketing classes at DePaul University since 2006, and the IBM Social Computing Guidelines have been indispensable in providing direction to students looking to meaningfully engage in business social media. To this excellent resource I now add another, Ed Brill's *Opting In*. The book is an honest and open combination of history and insight, in which Ed shares how he and IBM have used social media to make a technology giant more approachable and relevant to the lives of its customers and prospects. No small feat. The publishing industry abounds with social media guides at present. *Opting In* distinguishes itself from the completion by sharing real-world examples of what has worked (and what has not), with a clear explanation of the critical factors and lessons learned. Perhaps the new IBM meme will be 'Nobody ever got fired for 'Opting In'.'"
—**James Moore**
Director of Online Learning, DePaul University, Driehaus College of Business

"Many organizations are struggling to find ways to connect more effectively with their customers, partners, and their own employees. As an early adopter of social business solutions, IBM's Ed Brill has been excelling at this for more than a decade. In *Opting In*, he shares his experiences and insights on how to engage with communities and use their feedback to help guide critical business decisions. Anyone looking to learn how to leverage community feedback should put this on their reading list."
—**Alan Lepofsky**
Vice President and Principal Analyst, Constellation Research

"Social business is an organizational imperative. In *Opting In*, Ed Brill demonstrates how IBM transformed our culture and tools to connect people with people and insert social into business process. This book represents the best practices and lessons learned in an extremely effective, personal narrative. Must reading for any product or brand manager."
—**Jeff Schick**
Vice President, Social Software, IBM

"Ed has been involved with social software since its very early days, driving his personal, product, and corporate brand forward as the social landscape began to take shape. This book gives an insider's view of the evolution of the social business from a personal perspective and how brands needed to adapt to the changing way of communicating. He shows how the use of social media has enabled the growth of transparency in business and gives practical advice for aspiring social product managers. It is an excellent resource for any business wishing to activate its advocates and grow its agile social business."
—**Eileen Brown**
Contributor, Social Business column at ZDNet and author of *Working the Crowd: Social Media Marketing for Business*

"Clearheaded, actionable, and hype-free. As an IBM product manager who has successfully navigated the social business waters for himself, Ed demonstrates a remarkable ability to marry data and experience into a framework others can use to build, lead, and actualize social product strategies. This book is a must-read for any product manager with questions about navigating social business!"
—**Jason Seiden**
CEO, Ajax Workforce Marketing

"'Opting in' to become a more social business is imperative whether your business is large or small. This book gives you the roadmap you need to get there."
—**Laurie McCabe**
Partner, SMB Group

"Ed Brill's *Opting In* is an important book that takes social business beyond external marketing to provide practical guidance on how to drive significant business value through enhancing human interactions within the enterprise."
—**Bill Ives**
Partner, Merced Group

"Product management is a relationship business. It is about resonating with the user. *Opting In* shows you why and how social tools can accelerate relationships so you can sing to your consumer and make an extraordinary difference to the world."
—**Kantha Shelke**
Ph.D. Principal, Corvus Blue and developer who helped create and launch more than 100 food products that are still on the retail shelf today

Opting In

Opting In

Lessons in Social Business from a
Fortune 500 Product Manager

Ed Brill

IBM Press
Pearson plc

Upper Saddle River, NJ • Boston • Indianapolis • San Francisco
New York • Toronto • Montreal • London • Munich • Paris • Madrid
Cape Town • Sydney • Tokyo • Singapore • Mexico City

ibmpressbooks.com

IBM Press Program Managers: Steven M. Stansel, Ellice Uffer

Cover design: IBM Corporation

Associate Publisher: Dave Dusthimer
Marketing Manager: Dan Powell
Executive Editor: Mary Beth Ray
Publicist: Lisa Jacobson-Brown
Senior Development Editor: Christopher Cleveland
Managing Editor: Kristy Hart
Designer: Alan Clements
Peer Reviewers: Karen Lilla, Jeanne Murray, Jennifer Okimoto, Luis Suarez Rodriguez
Project Editor: Andy Beaster
Copy Editor: Keith Cline
Senior Indexer: Cheryl Lenser
Compositor: Nonie Ratcliff
Proofreader: Dan Knott
Manufacturing Buyer: Dan Uhrig

Published by Pearson plc
Publishing as IBM Press

IBM Press offers excellent discounts on this book when ordered in quantity for bulk purchases or special sales, which may include electronic versions and/or custom covers and content particular to your business, training goals, marketing focus, and branding interests. For more information, please contact

U. S. Corporate and Government Sales
1-800-382-3419
corpsales@pearsontechgroup.com.

For sales outside the U. S., please contact

International Sales
international@pearson.com.

Library of Congress Cataloging-in-Publication Data is on file.

Pearson Education, Inc.
Rights and Contracts Department
501 Boylston Street, Suite 900
Boston, MA 02116
Fax (617) 671 3447

ISBN-13: 978-0-13-325893-6

ISBN-10: 0-13-325893-9

Text printed in the United States on recycled paper at R.R. Donnelley in Crawfordsville, Indiana.
First printing January 2013

To my wife, Deborah, for inspiration, immeasurable patience,
and all of her support.

To my two beautiful daughters, M and C, for keeping me grounded
throughout this book project—and every day.

To those who believe in taking risks with me, professionally and personally.
Five career moves and many of my best memories have resulted
from someone taking a chance.
"Nothing ventured, nothing gained." Carpe diem.

Contents

Foreword   xv

Preface   xviii

Chapter 1 ▪ Why Social Business?   1
A Social Business Is Engaged   4
A Social Business Is Transparent   6
A Social Business Is Agile   7
Social Business and Earned Success   8
Lessons Learned   8
Endnotes   9

Chapter 2 ▪ The Social Product Manager   11
Enter the Social Product Manager   13
Analyzing an Analyst's Report   14
Social by Policy   20
Sales and Marketing Viewpoints   22
The Social Product Manager's Direct Feedback Loop   24
Lessons Learned   26
Endnotes   27

Chapter 3 ▪ Self, Product, or Company   27

Painting a Self-Portrait   30

Positioning Product   35

Representing the Company   41

Lessons Learned   44

Endnotes   45

Chapter 4 ▪ Offense or Defense   47

Situation Analysis   48

Timing   52

Volume and Amplification   55

Anticipation and Unintended Consequences   59

Lessons Learned   61

Endnotes   62

Chapter 5 ▪ Picking a Fight   63

You Can't Please All of the People...   64

Entering a Fray   68

Make Some Enemies   73

Lessons Learned   75

Endnotes   76

Chapter 6 ▪ Activate Your Advocates   77

Leadership   78

Content Versus Curation   78

Identifying Influencers and Providing Recognition   81

Continuous Feedback   85

Truth in Use   88

Lessons Learned   91

Endnotes   91

Chapter 7 ■ Tools of the Trade   93
2011 IBM CMO Study and the Importance
of Customer Insight   94
Inbound Social Networking Tools   95
Outbound Social Networking Tools   103
Forums and Feedback Sites   110
Lessons Learned   112
Endnotes   112

Chapter 8 ■ In Real Life   113
Amplify Your Message   114
Develop Community and Individual Relationships   116
Make Friends   123
Lessons Learned   127
Endnotes   128

Chapter 9 ■ Social Inside the Organization   129
Intersecting Organizational Goals and Social Tools   130
IBM as a Social Business   132
Measuring Return on Investment   138
The Impact of Social Tools on Product Development   140
Who Needs to Participate?   143
Lessons Learned   144
Endnotes   144

Chapter 10 ■ Risk Management in Social Business   145
Risk of Reaching the Wrong Audience   146
The Public Apology, and the Risk of Emotion   148
The Risk of Subset Population through Language
and Other Demographics   151
Risk of Identity Challenges and Imitations   152

Internal Risks   154

Lessons Learned   155

Endnotes   155

Chapter 11 ■   Putting *Opting In* into Practice   157

A Day in the Life   158

Using the "Lessons Learned"   160

The Social Product Manager of the Future   163

Next Steps   166

Conclusion   170

Appendix A ■   IBM Social Computing Guidelines   171

Introduction: Responsible Engagement in Innovation and
Dialogue   172

IBM Social Computing Guidelines   173

Detailed Discussion   174

Endnotes   179

Index   181

Foreword

Business has always been social. My grandmother learned practical strategies from workers she sold pencils to on the square of her Ukrainian hometown. My grandfather traded stock tips as he bought piece goods for the store he ran with his cousins in St. Louis decades later. Several thousand years of human culture, and my grandparents' personal stories, tell us people have always worked together, learned together, and helped one another succeed.

Yet recent popularity of the phrase "voice of the customer" implies that, for a long time, businesses stopped listening. As companies focused on efficiency and scale, big boom advertising drowned out other sounds. Human connection seemed soft. "It's all business" suggested calculating and cold.

Social media, now in the hands of millions, reintroduces a humanizing energy. Social tools amplify so many individual voices we can sound like the Hallelujah Chorus. Power generated by people, on our own and in self-organized groups, influences opinions and changes behavior. A Nielsen Global survey showed 90 percent of us make buying decisions based on relationships, over the influence of any other source.

Meanwhile I spend time working with companies to ensure that "voice of the employee" translates into "growing smarter from your world-class assets." Many business leaders act as if work would be easier if everyone would just quit talking so much. Some leaders apparently imagine soaring workplace productivity if people stopped attempting to learn from one another and make decisions based on trust. Why do people, individually, prove invaluable, yet people together signal trouble?

Social media tools designed specifically for use inside companies (also referred to as social business tools) are gaining momentum fast. They're still largely used, though, for communication and sharing, not yet replacing the outmoded business processes seen as the "real work." Perhaps they're not dreaded enough or seem too easy.

The tools themselves don't cause missed opportunity; rather, they're limited by old-style business culture. Even as groups form online and organize for action, leaders often see people within the work force as "parts" rather than pieces of an interlocking whole. Words and sentiment are analyzed rather than synthesized, tinkered with instead of valued as they illuminate collective brilliance in their midst.

Ed Brill lives at the seam of this dichotomy. He has transformed one of those big blocks of real work into a modern practice, where the voices of customers and employees mix. Managing products designed for collaborative work, he has developed a vast intra-enterprise network of people interested in the issues he toils over each day.

Beyond the independent blog he writes and idea jams he contributes to, other people's blog comments and status updates expand his optics into organizations he wouldn't otherwise see. There he recognizes product management works in similar ways as it did years ago. While knowing people expect to connect, product managers still struggle to make connections.

Ed's experience inside IBM, an organization transforming into a vibrant community of sharing, helped him realize he could serve as a lighthouse and a bridge.

In today's fast-paced marketplace, new technology must leap over years of incremental change. Inviting a network of stakeholders into the development cycle provides greater assurance products meet people's needs. As product managers contribute and listen, their marketplace leans in to hear perspectives and trade offs. Along the way they cultivate trust. As customers and prospects engage, they build momentum long before advertising engines rev up.

I've followed Ed's blog for years, and I'm consistently impressed with the variety, veracity, and value he assembles. He exemplifies the social business leader, connecting people, information, and insights, innovating every day.

If we look at Ed's approach as a blueprint for our own, even if our role isn't product management, we learn how to widen our reach. We see how to embrace everyone who may touch the products we work on. In doing so, we can finely tune our offerings to the needs and desires of the people who we serve.

Ed offers a window into a more inclusive world of mutual respect and understanding, in the face of a cynical merry-go-round of enticement and unmet expectations. He shows us the voice of the customer is also the voice of an employee, the voice of trusted allies, the voice of caring friends, and the voice we ought to listen for everywhere we go.

Opting In turns product management and marketing on its head, averting the need to sift through tea leaves as we attempt to discern what people want. When you read this book, you'll see actionable insights everywhere, gems to laugh with, savor, and share.

Opting In implores us to lean in to the conversation. By hearing what Ed's composing, we strengthen both our listening skills and our voices, speaking up for the opportunity to do exceptional work.

—Marcia Conner
Principal, SensifyWork
Staunton, Virginia
November 2012

Preface

Is social networking just the latest trendy management tool? Is social business the wave of the future or just an overused buzzword?

Most books on social business have focused on sales and marketing or on overall organizational change. The catalyst for writing *Opting In* was my belief, proven through a decade of real-world experience, that product management as a discipline significantly contributes to the fabric of a social business.

Of course, being social is not an automatic recipe for a successful product or service, nor is it even a necessary ingredient. However, as one of my IBM colleagues, Uffe Sørensen, often says, "The social conversation about your products/services is already taking place. Your only decision is whether as a vendor you want to be part of it."

There is an individual aspect to the decision as well. Clearly, a generational shift has taken place, as "digital natives" have entered the work force. Today, technology as a decision support tool has evolved beyond dashboards and spreadsheets. The expectation exists that tools for social and mobile collaboration will exist in the workplace. If the IT organization chooses to opt out, the lines of business will find ways to adopt social tools anyway.

Marcia Conner, author of *The New Social Learning* and the foreword for *Opting In,* once described the cultural change she witnessed at a particular organization. This company, extremely concerned about security, decided not only to prohibit access to public social networks from the company's computers but also to take possession of employee smartphones while the staff were inside the workplace.

After a few weeks of this policy, employees started taking longer lunch breaks. Observers noticed many of the staff simply sitting in their cars in the parking lot during their lunch breaks. Instead of running errands or grabbing a bite, the staff were using their smartphones for all the things that they were restricted from doing while "working."

CEOs and other senior organizational leaders have recognized the change in employee expectations. Where they are championing the cultural change to a social business, the profile of a successful employee is also changing.

Why do you want to be a social product manager? Because the attributes that make a successful product manager now turn out to be the most-desired talents *across the entire organization.* The agility, influence, leadership, and communication that personify a great product manager are now the characteristics that will excel in any role in any company.

The IBM CEO Study 2012 identified this trend:

Across industries and geographies, CEOs consistently highlight four personal characteristics most critical for employees' future success: being collaborative, communicative, creative and flexible. Given their intent to create greater openness, CEOs are looking for employees who will thrive in this kind of atmosphere.

However, we believe there's another driver behind the high ranking of this particular group of traits. For years, organizations have been embroiled in the so-called war for talent. The challenge has historically been a shortage of particular skills. But today, it's virtually impossible for CEOs to find the future skills they will need—because they don't yet exist. Bombarded by change, most organizations simply cannot envision the functional capabilities needed two or three years from now. Conventional training faces some of the same challenges. By the time courses are designed and delivered, the subject skills are already becoming outdated.

Instead, CEOs are increasingly focused on finding employees with the ability to constantly reinvent themselves. These employees are comfortable with change; they learn as they go, often from others' experiences. As a healthcare CEO from Australia explained, "Today's connected economy is full of ambiguity, and the characteristics required to navigate that ambiguity are collaboration, creativity and communication."[1]

In other words, the lessons of *Opting In* will help you differentiate yourself as an employee.

As a product or brand manager, you already possess the talents needed to succeed under any conditions. Product managers embody the principles of a social business: engaged, transparent, and agile.

Social product managers exemplify the skills of communication, collaboration, and coordination—the three C's—and can flourish in any situation. Social business provides the tools to move beyond gut instinct or lost cycle time waiting for traditional market research, incorporating more voices and providing insights across the entire organization. Social product managers are credible influencers on their organization and the market. They are more efficient at their jobs, and more successful at accomplishing their objectives.

My own career has been significantly impacted by the decision to engage with the market I made over a decade ago. New opportunities opened up at IBM because of my digital reputation and influence. The marketplace listened and participated, leading to opportunities to work with customers and prospects all over the world, and more success for the products I manage.

You can increase your individual potential and organizational success by incorporating the methods and tools discussed in *Opting In* on your product/brand management journey. You will influence more authoritatively and lead more effectively. You will increase awareness of your product or service and make it more successful. You will have more fun and make new contacts and friends. And you will remind yourself why you got into product management in the first place: to delight your customers and make a difference.

[1] IBM Institute for Global Business Value, IBM CEO Study 2012, "Leading Through Connections," May 2012, pages 20–21.

Acknowledgments

Writing a book is much more than putting words into sentences. *Opting In* has been an incredible learning process. Many people contributed to this effort, or to the journey that led here. I have attempted to list them all here, as a small way to express my appreciation and gratitude.

Thank you to my family—Deborah, M, and C—for their support and patience of all the late nights and weekends spent writing, and to the rest of my family for their encouragement and enthusiasm.

Opting In is the result of persistent persuasion by two wonderful IBM colleagues: Steve Stansel and Ellice Uffer. Thank you to both of you for creating this opportunity.

Many IBMers provided direct contributions, served as editors, offered advice, or otherwise helped make this book happen. Thank you to Karen Lilla, for one and a half times the effort through both editing and content guidance, along with peer editors Jennifer Okimoto, Jeanne Murray, and Luis Suarez Rodriguez. You elevated this book in so many ways.

Several other IBMers also provided valuable insights for this project: Ben Edwards, Patrick O'Donnell, Carolyn Baird, Ethan McCarty, Dana Anastasi, and Don Neely. My colleagues within the IBM Software Solutions executive team offered tremendous support for the book, including Mike Rhodin, Alistair Rennie, Jeff Schick, Sandy Carter, Kevin Cavanaugh, Bethann Cregg, Colleen Hayes, Brent Peters, and Bob McDonald. My staff were enthusiastic about this project and helped brainstorm specific concepts and examples, all of which was very much appreciated. Thanks, too, to my assistant, Jodi Corbett, though I suspect her workload from this project will increase once the first copy is printed.

Thank you to the direct contributors to the book: Marcia Conner, Joyce Davis, Bruce Elgort, Amy Hoerle, Brian O'Neill, Michael Sampson, Paul

Mooney, and Paul Withers. I have had the opportunity to work with Michael on two of his own books, and his personal advice was invaluable. One exception: Michael's suggestion to use a dictation process rather than typing out every one of these pages was a great concept, but as a visual thinker, I had to own every one of these words as they came out of my fingers and into the keyboard. Next time, Michael, I'll listen.

Many others graciously agreed to be quoted: Charlene Li, Olga Kozanecka, Dan Gillmor, Ross Mayfield, Jacob Share, Mary Beth Raven, Jeremy Hodge, Jake Ochs, Tim Tripcony, Tom Duff, Mikkel Heisterberg, Simon Vaughan, and Nathan Freeman. Several IBM marketers worldwide are unattributed contributors to *Opting In*, as content within drew upon existing published works and intranet pages. Thanks to all.

This book is based on a decade of living life online, and over that time, several people have served as partners, coaches, or supporters. Thank you to John Head and PSC Group LLC for hosting edbrill.com since 2003; Volker Weber for catalyzing and the initial blog hosting; Jacob Nelson and Libby Ingrassia, two editors who helped develop my writing and finally got me to stop double-spacing after a period.

Thank you to the team at Pearson Education: Mary Beth Ray, Christopher Cleveland, Dan Powell, Keith Cline, Andy Beaster, and several others, who made this rookie effort painless and professional.

Last, and most importantly, thank you to the entire "Lotus community." Whatever we call the products, those of you who "bleed yellow" are not just the subject of many of this book's stories, you are my friends and family. You have inspired me every day of the past two decades.

—Ed

About the Author

Ed Brill is Director, Product Management—IBM Social Business solutions.

Brill is responsible for the product and market strategy for IBM's messaging, collaboration, communications, and productivity products, including IBM Notes/Domino, IBM SmartCloud Notes, IBM Sametime, IBM Docs, and other related social business solutions. Brill's focus is on extending and growing the success of these solutions through customer engagement, partner ecosystem development, and harnessing the breadth and depth of the IBM organization.

In 18 years at IBM, Brill has led a variety of sales, marketing, and product-related organizations. As Director for Social Business, Brill has succeeded in elevating IBM's expertise and reputation in brand and product management. He has constantly innovated in both marketplace strategy and product execution.

Previously, during Brill's role as Business Unit Executive—Worldwide Sales, his suite of products posted year-to-year quarterly growth for four years and gained thousands of new customers. Earlier in his IBM career, Brill led competitive strategy and held several product management and strategic marketing roles. Brill's technical background includes development of infrastructure deployments through project management and IT architect roles.

Committed to understanding the global marketplace, Brill has visited IBM customers in more than 40 countries, and is a frequent speaker at IBM and industry events worldwide. Brill has served on the advisory boards for Web 2.0 Expo and IDG Mobile Enterprise Next.

Outside of IBM, Brill is an active Chicago community member. As a 25-year resident of Highland Park, Illinois, Brill authors "Highlands and

Ravines," a regular opinion column on community news website Patch.com, and previously wrote for the *Chicago Tribune*'s TribLocal.

Brill holds a Bachelor of Science degree in marketing from Indiana University, with a minor in political science.

Use the following to connect with the author online:

- **Blog**: www.edbrill.com, named a Best Blog for Buyers by Network World
- **Twitter:** http://twitter.com/edbrill
- **Facebook:** http://facebook.com/edbrilldotcom
- **LinkedIn**: http://linkedin.com/in/edbrill

I

Why Social Business?

The job of a product manager is to build a business plan for a product or service, then carry out the plan. Product managers assess what markets to serve, how to serve them, how to win, and for how long.

Today, there are new tools—and a new organizational mindset—that can make the product or brand manager more successful. This new approach brings new products to market faster, identifies opportunities for innovation, and anticipates changing market conditions.

The approach is called *social business,* an application of the concepts of social networking to encourage organizational cooperation and streamline challenges.

For most business leaders, the term **social networking** still conjures images of employees spending their valuable work time surfing Facebook and Twitter, chatting over Skype, or watching YouTube videos. It is a lingering loaded management question: What are our employees actually *doing,* should we be restricting or blocking it, and do these tools matter to anyone other than the marketing department?

A social business operates in ways that drive business value through optimized human interaction. Within the organization, people apply relevant content and expertise to ideas, activities, and output, the result of cultural change and technology adoption that encourages the sharing of knowledge and insights. The result is a transformed business that is highly participatory, makes informed decisions, and cultivates loyalty among employees and customers.

Although success is about more than the tools, most conversations about social business lead to marketing today. Many organizations have set up or hired an online presence on the major social networks, have community managers in their marketing department, and are using social media to drive advertising or marketing campaigns. Internally, many companies use collaboration tools to increase organizational communication and knowledge sharing. However, only a small percentage have envisaged a complete embrace and adoption of social business.

In her book *Get Bold,* IBM Vice President Sandy Carter writes:

Social Business leverages all the social tools and techniques of social media, but expands the usage and efficiencies beyond "media and marketing" to all of a company's processes, both internal and external.

At IBM, we believe that social business represents the fifth wave of computing. Just as the mainframe, PC, client/server, and Internet eras all represented transformational moments in both business and technology, social business is an inflection point in how organizations leverage their relationships—internally and externally—to be more successful.

To truly realize the full potential of a social business, leaders also need to empower a company's most vital asset: its people.

Consider some attention-grabbing data points:

- IBM's 2012 CEO Study of more than 1,700 chief executive officers from 64 countries and 18 industries worldwide reveals that only 16 percent of CEOs are using social business platforms to connect with customers, but that number is poised to spike to 57 percent within the next three to five years.
- IBM's 2011 CIO Survey of 3,000 global leaders indicated that more than 55 percent of companies identified social networking as having a strategic significance to their company's growth.

- According to Pew Research, 66 percent of online adults use social networking sites. Generationally, Pew has identified that **millennials**—people born between 1981 and 2000—"will make online sharing in networks a lifelong habit."[1] As millennials have entered the workforce, they have brought this trait with them, and expect the same of colleagues and clients.

In other words, social business isn't some hot new fad that will be over in an Internet minute. In the consumer space, examples abound of how social media isn't something companies can opt out of. Traditional ways of managing the message no longer apply. Bloggers, chat boards, e-shopping and ratings sites, and specialized forums all offer any buyer information about their intended purchase at the click of a Google search.

But social business is bigger than that. The transformational opportunity is more than watching online product demonstrations, comparing commodity prices, or checking hotel ratings. Social business utilizes the same methods of crowdsourcing, interactivity, immediacy, and relational linking, applied to a broader set of content and networks. Social business is a way of thinking, a discipline, a cultural change.

Within the discipline of product or brand management, social business provides a significant opportunity. *Opting In* explores ways to apply the concepts of social business specifically to building products and services. In these eleven chapters, you will learn both the why and how of becoming a social product manager—a thought leader, an insightful decision maker, and an open communicator.

The concepts and examples throughout the book illustrate the daily activities of product management through the lens of three core characteristics, attributes embraced throughout the organization:

- **Engagement:** Deeply connecting people, including customers, employees, suppliers, partners, influencers, and even competitors, resulting in productive, efficient communication and sharing.
- **Transparency:** Removing boundaries to information, experts, and assets, resulting in increased alignment, confidence, and comprehension.
- **Agility:** Utilizing information and insight to anticipate and address evolving opportunities, resulting in faster decisions and increased responsiveness.

Throughout *Opting In,* I tie back to these three characteristics often, because they are the core principles of how to leverage social business. They are not as simple as they sound on the surface; to apply these traits to a business, especially a large or public company, requires significant cultural change. The social product manager can lead, influence, or follow such a transformation, but must adapt one or more of these core concepts. Often a product manager's focus on one of these characteristics results in the emergence of all three, laying the foundation for success in social business.

A Social Business Is Engaged

Engaged sounds the most straightforward of the three. Engaged is a baseline choice—will you participate in the market or not? A company cannot be a social business without being engaged, but this does not necessarily imply direct participation.

A well-known example of a company that eschews social media is Apple. Its employees do not blog, post, or tweet in any capacity related to their day jobs. Apparently, they are not utilizing foursquare, a location-based social networking service, either.

On foursquare, the person who has used a smartphone to "check in" at a particular place most frequently over the past 60 days is crowned "mayor." Much to my surprise, I briefly earned the mayoral title at Apple's corporate campus in Cupertino, California, after only two days of meetings there in May 2010.

Although I was initially surprised at the dubious honor, I realized that Apple's complete corporate silence on social networks was to blame. The Twitter ID @Apple has more than 6,000 followers, but no profile information and has never tweeted. The Apple, Inc., page on Facebook has more than 6.5 million likes, after only a year on the service. Despite the opportunity to reach and engage loyal customers, instead the Apple page only displays postings from your friends.

Yet Apple recognizes the value of social business. On apple.com, Apple support communities are among the site's most-visited web pages, with more than one million discussion threads started in the past four years.

Because support forums rely on active participation of knowledgeable experts to supply answers, Apple has provided several social incentives for contributions. Forum participants have individual profiles and can customize that profile to provide public information about their background, expertise, and interests. Each time a participant posts in the forum, the post is accompanied by their "level" and "points" on the Apple forum. Score points are earned from other participants; ten points for each "this solved my question" acknowledgment, and five points for each "this helped me" vote. There may or may not be any kind of reward involved in a system like this; for many community participants, the badge of pride associated with a high score or level is recognition enough.

For Apple, providing a self-service community drastically reduces the customer support burden that the company bears directly for its products. Consumers assist each other with product questions, configuration, requests, and even defects. Customer satisfaction is actually increased because answers in the forums address not just the person who originally asked the question but also the next consumer with the same question, forming a knowledge base built up over years. Participants in the forum feel more loyal and connected to Apple because they have been able to share knowledge and earn recognition in an affiliated way, on the pages of Apple's own property.

How does a self-service forum support the concept of being engaged? I can't speak for Apple, but I can say that at IBM we also host numerous forums on the pages of ibm.com. We monitor those forums for hot topics and trends, and use those as inputs into the product development and support process. If a question is arising often, it can be converted into an FAQ (frequently asked questions) document, technical support note, or added to our product documentation. Forum contributions often include best practices or tips, which we can incorporate into product improvements or documentation.

Another valuable aspect of forum discussions is that they often go off-topic into overall marketplace discussions. Over the years, I have found myself in online conversations about market share, competitive positioning, and business partner solutions for my products as a result of discussions on ibm.com forums. I discuss the importance, and the balance, of having marketplace discussions in public in Chapter 6, "Activate Your Advocates".

Although the preceding examples are organizational in nature, engagement applies to individuals as well. Those who engage are people, making individual decisions within the framework of their company culture and orientation toward social business.

Engaged product managers, as discussed in the chapters ahead, have the opportunity to individually lead and influence the market, help connect people to people, and increase their own knowledge and confidence. Social product managers are constantly engaged, inside and outside their organization.

A Social Business Is Transparent

Transparency as a social business concept is the hardest one for line managers and business executives to embrace. I discuss this concept often throughout *Opting In;* the very premise of opting in to social business discussions is the notion that communicating openly takes work but provides rewards. In product management, transparency is a challenging notion because brand managers and leaders are always building the future. It might be too early to discuss plans openly, lest they fall into competitors' hands or prematurely influence customer (current or prospective) decision making. Inside an organization, transparency flies in the face of traditional corporate instinct to protect one's knowledge as the source of the individual's unique value to the company.

Being transparent is a key behavior in social business transformation. Several years ago, a professional services organization I worked with took its first step toward being a social business when a new CEO came onboard. Previously, organizational strategy and vision had been communicated through traditional methods, including memos, company meetings, and other asynchronous tools. The new CEO decided that he would rather use a blog (web log) to share his new ideas. Associates within the organization quickly learned that it was acceptable, even encouraged, to comment on the ideas shared by the CEO on his blog. The CEO received significant, immediate, and candid feedback on those ideas, and the employees internalized the strategic communications because of their ability to participate in a conversation.

One unintended consequence developed out of this transparency: Employees in the organization realized that the CEO was reading their comments on his blog and used the opportunity to completely flatten their internal communication structure. Topics on the CEO's blog were routinely "hijacked" with new discussion themes in attempts to raise other issues to the CEO. After some time, the CEO provided a new vehicle for internal advocacy, which he called "the speaker's corner" after the venue in London's Hyde Park. The off-topic discussions migrated to the new tool, and the CEO once again had the ability to engage in timely strategic discussions with the entire organization.

Transparency has the advantage of bringing people into conversations they might not otherwise be exposed to. It flattens an organization and leads to better information flow. Being transparent often introduces a new cultural element to many organizations—that of admitting and discussing when something goes wrong. Transparency often encourages a culture of continuous improvement rather than always striving to get things right the first time.

A Social Business Is Agile

The third concept, being nimble, ties in nicely with that thought of continuous improvement. In modern times, with petabytes of information available in real time and innovation often being the only differentiator among competitors, agility is a key attribute to success. Therefore, nimble organizations anticipate opportunities, adjust to market conditions rapidly, and are willing to reconsider approaches and decisions. Agility means putting an end to typically off-limits organizational norms and truisms in favor of fact-based decisions, and is the area where analytical tools are best applied to understand market sentiment and desire.

Agility often accompanies crisis management. In late 2010, retailer The Gap unveiled a new logo. The new wordmark utilized a standard sans serif font, with a small blue box to pay homage to the previous company image. Within minutes, the new logo was labeled a failure. Consumer sentiment on blogs, Twitter, and Facebook ran extremely negative, and the company was forced to retreat. Though at the time they indicated some intent to try to re-imagine the logo, even soliciting consumer participation, two years later the logo remains the same as it was going back to the early 1990s.

At the time, some speculated that the new logo was a publicity stunt and that there was never an intention to truly change the Gap image. However, the company's public statements—which, innovatively, they published in places such as the Huffington Post—made clear this was just genuinely a bad decision. They were transparent and nimble, and the crisis passed.

Agility isn't just about crisis management. One of the very first successful social business examples originated almost two decades ago. In 1990, American car manufacturer Chrysler Corporation implemented a Supplier Cost Reduction Effort (SCORE) program, which encouraged vendors to provide recommendations to the manufacturer on how to save money. The suppliers received a share of the savings from any of their ideas that were implemented, which created a culture of trust and transparency. In the mid-1990s, Chrysler moved the SCORE program online, utilizing a collaboration software program and open discussions. With greater participation, thousands of proposals were received, and billions of dollars were saved as a result of quickly implementing supplier ideas.

Social Business and Earned Success

This first chapter has utilized broad, well-known companies—rather than IBM or personal stories—as examples to familiarize you with the characteristics of a social business. Each of these cases demonstrates the success of acting in an open, agile, and connected manner. Today, many marketers are talking about paid, owned, and earned media. For working with customers, suppliers, and partners, traditional methods—paid media advertising and communication and owned properties such as corporate websites—are fast being supplanted by earned media, where those external parties are the voice and the channel. This is where most social media tomes spend their time and energy, and clearly earned media is a critical component of the marketing mix today. These same three concepts apply to organizational behavior now, too. Owned media is evolving to encompass new forms of owned communications, such as vendor blogs and infographics. Earned has emerged as increasingly influential, with employees at all organizational levels choosing to participate in thought leadership, horizontal communication, and transparent activity. Now is the time to understand how these new methods of behavior, new models of culture, and new tools of collaboration all combine to make a social business a successful business.

Lessons Learned

- Social business is a broader subject matter than social media; social business is a cultural transformation of an organization and its relationships with customers, suppliers, partners, and the marketplace.
- Social business, while trendy, is not a fad that can be ignored. Organizations must opt in to social business as a key component of innovation, best practice, and understanding the market.

- Social businesses adopt a range of tools and cultural changes to become more engaged, transparent, and agile. Both technology and organizational adaptation are required to be successful, but the process can be gradual and iterative.

Endnotes

[1] Pew Internet, "Millennials will make online sharing in networks a life-long habit," Janna Anderson/Lee Rainie, July 2010 (http://tinyurl.com/388y5pg).

2

The Social Product
Manager

Different organizations define the role of a product manager in diverse ways, but the core job responsibility is to manage the lifecycle of product and service offerings—things a company sells to customers. From concept to introduction to maturity, product or brand managers are responsible for the care and feeding of their solutions, making key strategic decisions that result in success or failure.

Product management is a fascinating discipline. Waking up every morning to new challenges, market conditions, innovations, and having to make sense of it all is demanding yet exciting. The decisions made by product managers affect every other part of an organization, yet the product manager often has no direct responsibility over the other contributing functions within the organization. **Influence,** therefore, becomes a strong unit of currency for successful product managers.

In the fast-paced technology industry, many product managers believe it is an instinctive role, where good product managers are born, not made. Technology product managers often employ gut reaction and a crystal ball as key tools for decision making. In some segments of the market, the product lifecycle is so short that this is the only potentially successful approach; there is no time to validate, verify, or build affinity. There is also the constant challenge of uncharted waters; many technology products are first-movers or inventing a new category.

At IBM, we prefer an approach where decisions are made by consensus and supported by data, though we still leave some room for creativity and inclination. IBM's integrated product development process drives the product management lifecycle, with rigorous checkpoints and functional requirements. However, recognizing that flexibility is a key factor to success, IBM product managers have a broad spectrum of tools at their disposal to design and change products or services, and to obtain feedback on key product attributes or messages throughout the design and development process.

In business school decades ago, I learned that the tools of marketing included focus groups, surveys, feedback forms, and other types of market research. The textbooks were filled with case studies of poorly researched products that did not succeed simply because the producer had misunderstood their opportunity or the market. My first marketing class studied the introduction of chicken hot dogs by poultry producer Perdue Farms in 1984. The product failed for a variety of reasons.

In 2013, though, Perdue could dominate the market segment. Today, introducing the concept under a different name—gourmet chicken sausages, which now line the meat departments of every major supermarket in North America—would ensure success for Perdue's chicken hot dogs.

The university case study hypothesized that Perdue misunderstood the market opportunity and simply missed out on how to market their new product.

Perhaps a social product manager could have avoided failure when Perdue introduced chicken hot dogs. The opportunity to instantly discuss the product's appeal or challenges with a broad segment of consumers did not exist at the time. The tools available to Perdue did not help them identify the type of consumer who, even in the late 1980s, would have been interested in a healthful product, or to make the recipe changes to position it more as an upscale choice—something Perdue already did with its chicken.

While changing eating habits have certainly contributed to the success of the encased meats category today, had Perdue positioned the chicken hot dogs as a premium product in the first place, they might have led the category for decades.

There is still absolutely a place for formal market research and understanding in today's product manager toolkit. At Google, a cultural requirement for fact-based decision making has lead to reliance on A/B testing for validation. An A/B test uses selective sampling and testing to determine whether specific decisions will drive consumer behavior. Google conducted more than 7,000 A/B tests on its search algorithm during 2011 in an effort to optimize results. This approach to testing theories can be overdone; former Google engineers report being asked to conduct A/B tests on mundane topics such as pixel width of a table border.[1]

I believe product management is art as well as science. Although the data can always be manufactured to support a particular position, the creative process of innovation and outsmarting the competition often requires more than focus groups or A/B tests. There is risk taking involved in making smart decisions, especially when there is no time to collect data or conduct research.

Successful product managers can synthesize data and distill it to its essence; the gut instinct can be exercised and honed. Sometimes, product management is about making an educated guess rather than a data-driven decision. The question then is, how do you fulfill the "educated" part?

Enter the social product manager.

Enter the Social Product Manager

The social product manager leverages the collective knowledge and understanding of the marketplace to develop timely insights and make educated decisions. The social product manager understands how consumers, colleagues, and even competitors can be involved to fill gaps in knowledge that lead to faster and better decision making. Social product managers leverage their networks and ecosystem to support and encourage the right decisions. They use the most human of characteristics, **community**, to build success.

Most readers will find little to argue with in the preceding paragraph. Every brand manager wants to make the right decisions based on informed positions that will lead to success. What makes a social product manager different?

To answer this, recall the previous chapter's examination of the core characteristics of a social business: engaged, transparent, and agile. Some background on how IBM changed its culture completely to become a social business is also useful. There is also a personal motivation; many of the attributes that make a great product manager are the building blocks for a successful social product manager.

My first job in high school was the weekend shift at Burger King. Even then, I had a strong sense of believing in my product and standing up to the competition. My father incessantly teases me about my early loyalty. I refused during that time to eat at McDonald's, blindly declaring the superiority of the flame-broiled Whopper.

When I entered the professional workforce, I found myself initially in a job with no conviction. My project and the environment made no sense. I left, feeling that the only way I would be successful was to personally be confident in my objectives, both on an individual and business level. I learned quickly that my work style often gravitated to consensus building; that is, I enjoyed the intellectual nature of discussing and debating ideas and opportunities. This was "social" before social business was defined. Technology emerged to support the concepts, and I was an early adopter.

A decade ago, I began a blog on my own website, edbrill.com, as an outlet for creative energy and a way to connect with friends online in a broader way. After a year or so, I realized that the fastest way to build an audience for my blog was to write about topics related to my work as an IBM product manager. Sure, I enjoyed writing about other topics, but the blog posts that garnered the most visits, responses, and links were those related to my product or its marketplace.

Blogging initially appealed to my sense of fair play, truth and accuracy, and a little bit of competitive aggression. Suddenly, battling in the collaboration software marketplace was no longer the realm of off-the-record conversations and clandestine product analysis; transparency online could change the game.

The intersection of my particular product management responsibility at the time I started blogging—competitive intelligence—and the openness of the medium formed a powerful megaphone. The power to put the absolute truth in the light of day, for customers, prospects, and the competition to see, suddenly changed the dynamics of the battlefield.

Within 18 months of launching edbrill.com, this power was proven out.

Analyzing an Analyst's Report

In the software industry, we often utilize industry analyst white papers— short reports about our product or solution, extolling its benefits—as marketing material. Sometimes, these are general analyst reports that happen to support a particular product or vendors, whereas others are specifically commissioned by a vendor to recommend their solution. Analysts lend their expertise and credibility, along with market insight, to the published paper, which helps inform decision makers on how to choose the right product (or avoid the wrong one).

In the collaboration software marketplace, the Radicati Group is an analyst firm that authors both primary and sponsored research. Radicati Group had written several papers comparing an IBM solution with a Microsoft® product since the inception of the market in the 1990s. Radicati Group, like most analysts, made their living by selling these published reports, usually for thousands of dollars a copy.

Sometimes, vendors would sponsor or license a particular Radicati Group report, usually making it available publicly at no charge. One such Radicati report, the "Corporate Messaging Market Analysis," appeared on microsoft.com in July 2004, a few weeks after its publication. Unsurprisingly, the report was weighted heavily in favor of Microsoft's position and future success in the market, at the expense of IBM. It was, unfortunately, also inaccurate in several places, and contained a significant amount of hyperbole rather than solely being based on facts.

Before the inception of blogging, IBM would have had to simply accept a sucker punch like this report, as protests often drew more attention to the skirmish than the initial document. The glowing write-up would land in the inboxes of CIOs and decision makers everywhere, with nothing to refute the third-party endorsement.

Blogging changed all that. On July 23, 2004, I published a blog entry acknowledging the report's existence—an unusually engaged and transparent step for IBM as a vendor. I did not offer an opinion on the report myself, instead indicating that an official rebuttal would soon be published on IBM's website.

In my posting, I linked to another blog, that of Michael Sampson, an industry analyst in New Zealand who followed the marketplace closely and was highly respected. Sampson had undertaken a section-by-section refutation of the Radicati Group report, using public information and his own viewpoint in combination to skillfully combat the assertions of the Radicati report. I invited edbrill.com readers to join in the discussion of the report and the counteranalysis on Sampson's website.

What happened over the next ten days was an early demonstration of how the blogosphere would come to influence factual discussion, news, and debate.

On my own site, discussion of the report continued. Recognizing the sensitivity of the topic, I limited my comments to the facts; however, I clearly encouraged discussion regarding the report, both on the blog site itself and through private emails and chats.

The notion of product manager influence was on display, as those who trusted me—or were learning to do so through this particular episode of transparency—believed their voices were relevant to add to the conversation. This was not a blog topic that would simply fade in a day or two.

The Radicati Group contacted me via email to try to dispute some of the points of Michael Sampson's refutation, along with other comments that had been made about their report on other blogs. When I offered to publish their email on edbrill.com, though, they declined. On July 27, 2004, I decided to let the readers on my site know that this series of events had taken place.

In the comments in response to the July 27 entry, someone identifying himself only as Keiot attacked me personally, supporting the Radicati Group white paper's position while ascribing his supporting evidence to me as an individual. Perhaps Keiot did not understand the transparency of the Internet, though. I was able to quickly trace Keiot's comments to the same Internet address as the Radicati Group, and the screen name to the name of someone employed by Radicati Group at the time. I acknowledged this link in comments on my site, and suddenly the blogosphere—well beyond my normal reach—exploded.

SearchDomino.com published a story called "[U]sers fuming over Radicati report," while eWeek columnist Sean Gallagher wrote a blog entry called "When analysts Astroturf," referring to a fake grassroots effort. There were calls to my management, demanding my termination, and letters to then-IBM Chairman Sam Palmisano from supposedly angry shareholders.

Before blogging, I would have been standing accused all by myself. My crime was exposing a potentially erroneous report in the bright light of the truth. The analyst firm and Microsoft themselves were unprepared for that counteraction when Microsoft licensed and published the report; they simply expected it to be held up as an endorsement.

Instead, the high-tech industry, as if as one, sided with the truth. Vendors with no skin in the game commented on the skirmish. Ross Mayfield, then CEO of Socialtext and now vice president of Business Development at Slideshare, a LinkedIn company, noted the change in how the industry game was being played, stating, "This kind of back and forth used to occur in email, but now its public and impacts influence."[2]

The Radicati Group analyst firm, and their 2004 report, lived on. However, the inaccuracies of that report attracted so much unwanted attention that the report was tainted in the eyes of many of the decision makers that Microsoft had hoped to influence.

Coincidentally, nationally recognized columnist Dan Gillmor published his book *We the Media* just days after the dispute with Radicati Group. Gillmor's book resonated with me as the inflection point for a new era of open communication between vendors and customers, customers and customers, and in industry as a whole.

> *{W}e must all recognize that the rules for newsmakers, not just journalists, have changed, thanks to everyone's ability to make the news. ...*
>
> *Newsmakers need to understand that the swirling eddies of news are not tiny pools on the shoreline. Information is an ocean, and newsmakers can no longer control the tide as easily as they once did.*
>
> *So they must face at least three new rules of public life.*
>
> *First, outsiders of all kinds can probe more deeply into newsmakers' businesses and affairs. They can disseminate what they learn more widely and more quickly. And it's never been easier to organize like-minded people to support, or denounce, a person or cause. The communications-enabled grassroots is a formidable truth squad.*
>
> *Second, insiders are part of the conversation. Information no longer leaks. It gushes, through firewalls and other barriers, via instant messages, emails, and phone calls.*
>
> *Third, what gushes forth can take on a life of its own, even if it's not true.*[3]

In 2005, Dr. Sara Radicati, CEO of Radicati Group, told her side of the story to *Forbes* magazine, in a story titled "Attack of the Blogs!"[4] She claimed that her firm was "deluged" with negative feedback in an attempt to "disable [her] business." Ironically, the *Forbes* story itself became the target of much negativity and vitriol among social media experts, as if *Forbes* was attempting to cling to the old style of reporting where the media controlled the message.

MICHAEL SAMPSON ON GETTING CAUGHT OUT FOR POOR TRANSPARENCY

I believe that people who can make a strong argument based on a robust analysis of a market space, and a good understanding of the vendors, the offerings, and the pros and cons of the same, should be listened to. Often they have opportunities to study things that the general population don't have, and bring a particular analytical mindset to the future of IT strategy. I'm also firmly of the opinion that these conditions are not always met among the IT analysts of the world, both at a junior level and sometimes even by pieces of work that are stamped with larger names. I've heard anecdotally that decisions made inside organizations were made because a particular analyst at a certain company said what should be done, and so the business manager said, "We will do what they say." I think that line of approach shows an immaturity on the behalf of business managers, and signals that the analysts involved have too much power over decision making.

It was in light of these beliefs that in 2003–2005, when I came across pieces of analyst research that I felt inaccurately portrayed the market space, or had poor reasoning, or the numbers didn't stack up against other published numbers, that in response I wrote a blog post decrying the lack of analysis and analytical rigor that had been applied in the work. Sometimes it was also me questioning whether the work was a truly independent piece of work from an analyst firm, in which case it should be listened to at a different level, compared to research that was sponsored by the vendor for whom the analyst came out in favor of. This happened a couple of times when the work was portrayed as being independent, but it didn't pass the smell test for an independent piece.

In one of the blog posts I wrote decrying a particular analyst report, my blog post was picked up and linked to by a number of other people in the wider community who agreed with the position I was taking or merely linked to it out of interest. What started happening was that somebody, under a variety of names, started posting very critical comments about the analysis in my blog post. Now that's par for the course when you question something that someone else has done, but when a number of us started comparing notes, and in particular the IP address from which they were coming from, they all pointed back to a particular address. What we believed happened is that the lead author of the report in question was leaving comments on the various blogs under a variety of false names and attacking the point of view. Such discourse was allowed—it would even be welcomed—had it been under the person's actual name. The problem was in using a series of pseudonyms and in trying to muddy the waters about their involvement in the work. The whole thing turned into a firestorm and resulted in a write up in *Forbes* magazine called "The Attack of the Blogs."

There were lingering impacts of this activity for some time on the Internet. Searches for the analyst company's name turned up the whole sordid affair, which had a less-than-positive effect on their business reputation. I'm sure the vendors involved directly, as well as those watching the event from the sidelines, treaded more carefully about trying to make sponsored research look independent and pure. Call it what it is, but don't try to pass off one for the other. Finally, I think the event and the background story hurt the IT analyst business as a whole, calling its ethics and approach into question. If analysts are independent advisors to organizations, but are able to be bought off by the vendors through sponsored research, it's a sham—and I think that's bad, because analysts can have an essential role to play as trusted advisors.

To this date, I'm still shocked at what transpired in response to my blog post, and part of me still doesn't believe it happened. But when you look back at the blogs that were involved at the time, the comments are still there. The lesson should be clear: By all means be involved and even take hard positions, but you have to do so as yourself, not as someone you are pretending to be.

Michael Sampson is a Collaboration Strategist with the Michael Sampson Company. August 2012, used with permission.

The publication of the inaccurate Radicati Group report, and its subsequent online dissection, changed the nature of competition in the messaging marketplace. Sponsored or licensed analyst reports were effectively neutralized as a tool in the competitive battle. No vendor could expect an opinion-based third-party endorsement to stand up in the marketplace.

Although I might handle some of the conflict with Radicati Group differently if it all were to happen today, the entire skirmish embodied important principles of a social product manager. I used the truth as an absolute defense. I stuck to facts. I was honest. I was transparent. The facts inspired others to join the discussion and amplify the story.

Internally at IBM, I kept my management informed throughout the encounter with the Radicati Group report, from the day it was posted on Microsoft's website to the last posting on the topic. With most of the discussion taking place on public blogs, anyone could examine the facts, the approach, and the tone of the discourse.

Social by Policy

About a year later, many of the principles of conduct discussed earlier in this chapter became policy at IBM. In a watershed case of internal empowerment, a group of IBM employees (including me) worked together in early 2005 to write blogging guidelines for use by all IBMers. The contributors came initially from rank and file line of business, not—as you might expect—from human resources, or legal, or finance. An internal wiki was used to author and edit the draft policy, allowing anyone with an opinion or example to contribute to the effort.

Note

A wiki is a freely editable web page, one of the essential social networking tools (for example, Wikipedia, a crowdsourced wiki publication).

The blogging guidelines, which are now called the IBM Social Computing Guidelines, represented a turning point for IBM culturally. They were written to *encourage*, rather than discourage, engagement. Unlike most policy documents, which function as boundaries for conduct, the social computing guidelines say:

> {I}t is very much in IBM's interest—and, we believe, in each IBMer's own— to be aware of and participate in this sphere of information, interaction, and idea exchange.

The entire IBM Social Computing Guidelines are included in *Opting In* as Appendix A. IBM has published them externally since they were first approved in 2005, because we believe they represent part of our commitment to clients and the marketplace, as well as an example of a best practice we can share with other organizations. Only twice in the past seven years have they been updated, mainly to take into consideration new technology platforms. The concepts have stood the test of time.

What the written document doesn't embody is the cultural change that went along with it. That cultural change is important to the success of the social product manager because it supports the behavior, the thought of being engaged, transparent, and agile.

When I became part of IBM in 1995, I still had residual images of the company as a faceless conglomerate, blue suits and white shirts and red ties and wingtips, all left over from a college campus interview sequence in the late 1980s. Elements of that culture remained part of the company for many years. Even just a decade ago, IBM had a sentiment that avoided significant recognition of individual employees. In a 2003 blog entry, I referred to someone who had just been named as general manager of one of our divisions; my corporate communications team reached out within an hour and reminded me that "we don't have celebrities at IBM."

We still don't have celebrities, but the Social Computing Guidelines changed the culture of identity at IBM. For the first time, employees were allowed—encouraged—to contribute to the conversation, utilizing their own individual names as brands. IBMers were suddenly able to demonstrate the incredible breadth and depth of the organizational knowledge and expertise we possessed internally. Suddenly, there were three elements to our external messages: self, product, and company. Chapter 3, "Self, Product, or Company," explores this thought in more detail.

The guidelines accomplished one other major transformational element that enabled IBM to become a social business. They signaled—to employees, clients, and the market—that IBM would stand behind its employees. Over the decade in which I have operated as a social product manager, the IBM chairman's office has received three complaints about content I have authored publicly. Each time, because I complied with the Social Computing Guidelines, IBM has backed me, confirming that what I wrote was in line with what the company believes to be good corporate citizenship.

The successful social product manager needs to be able to spread their influence with the confidence that their organization to uphold their individual positions and statements. Social business is not just about adopting technology and tools, although these are obviously important elements. Just as important are the policy and cultural requirements that must exist, or be adopted, as transformational elements, from the very top of an organization. This is as certain for internal use of social business tools as it is for external.

Empowering employees to collaborate and share knowledge and expertise has a tendency to change the power dynamics within an organization. The value of an individual's role to the company is no longer defined by the knowledge that person accrues, but instead by the way in which the individual shares it. People become identified for their expertise and influence, not just their title or reporting structure. Management must be prepared to grant and encourage visibility and participation for their employees, at an individual level.

We have changed so much at IBM that we recently ran a series of advertisements identifying individual IBMers and their expertise. The "I'm an IBMer" ads[5] were the strongest signal possible to the market—and also to our employees—that individual voices are what makes our organization great.

The social product manager does not always need to be the mouthpiece, though. In my organization today, I have a staff consisting of both extroverts and introverts. Those who do not participate can still be social product managers, just by listening. The individual voices from the marketplace can be synthesized and distilled, without having everyone speaking out loud.

Some of our most productive engagements and results come from situations where my team participates in listen-only mode, much like the concept of sitting behind the one-way mirror watching a focus group. This behavior is no less "social"; it is an important empowerment for those who believe their role is driven by influence and results, not necessarily by volume.

Social product managers will find an affinity for their voice in certain functional areas of the organization, and some opposition to their transparency and agility in others. The sales organization typically adores the social product manager, for sharing information broadly and establishing expertise. Tensions will exist with other marketing functions, including product marketing and communications departments, because of traditional notions of timing and "launching" the release of information.

Sales and Marketing Viewpoints

Salespeople make the best consumers of my social business content, whether it is posted publicly on my blog or on Twitter or Facebook or on IBM's own Connections social business platform. (I talk more about Connections in Chapter 7, "Tools of the Trade.") Salespeople thrive on product information. Their job is, after all, to inform customers on products and solutions. Therefore, the more they know about what we offer now and in the future, the more successful they will be.

Salespeople are often just-in-time information consumers, so search engines are their friend. It actually surprised me how many IBMers were using my public content from edbrill.com and elsewhere in their conversations with customers. This ability to reach a broad internal audience actually increased my propensity to share. Why send emails blindly hoping to reach the right people, when instead a single blog post or tweet or internal wiki entry can reach thousands?

The content opens a channel, too. Over the years, I've received countless emails that started "I read on your blog...." The social product manager can prompt leads and opportunities, sometimes months or years after content creation. The mere act of sharing conveys to readers that you are willing to be engaged on a particular topic, breaking down barriers that normally inhibit finding the right expertise. The result of many of those emails is the direct opportunity to speak to customers or prospects, or learn more about opportunities, which at the end of the day is what drives the business forward.

One area of your organization that may be less excited about the transparent and agile nature of social business, surprisingly given how strongly these functions have adopted social *media,* is marketing and communications. These functional areas have been turned upside down by social tools; suddenly, everyone is a content creator, and widespread distribution of information can be accomplished with a single click. The tools themselves run the risk of disintermediating the people whose jobs are to tell your story to the market, so the cultural aspects of adopting social business are more important here than the technology.

Within the past year, we at IBM have been building a number of tools for mobile collaboration, specifically for use on iPads and other tablets. Understandably, everyone gets excited about shiny new toys for these devices, and the natural tendency is to want to show off. When the first release of our IBM Connections app for mobile devices was completed, the social product managers were off and running. There were tweets, blog posts, internal forum postings, and other general excitement within hours of product completion sign-off.

Only one problem: Although the app was quickly available on Google Play and the Blackberry App World, the process of clearing the new release for Apple's App Store was taking longer. All three app stores allow vendors to submit new applications with an intended release date, but nobody had thought to plan for such a coordinated event. The excitement of the new app overtook traditional marketing needs to amplify a coordinated message.

Understandably, the communications team within IBM was not amused by all the social buzz created for the new application—before it was available to be downloaded by iPhone and iPad users or, for that matter, reporters. The opportunity to present the story of our new application to journalists and the market was already lost, as word was out through social tools. Further, customers who read the uncoordinated communications became frustrated when seeking the new application on the Apple App Store, finding nothing available.

In the ensuing fray, it was recognized that an opportunity had been missed. To preserve any hope of attracting mainstream press attention, it was necessary to put the genie back in the bottle. This was no easy task—nor was it particularly authentic or transparent in an age of instant publication. But blogs were rescinded, tweets were deleted, and links were broken. IBM's communication team took the reins and coordinated a launch date for a formal press release, social media outreach, and marketing activities. The resulting press coverage in the mainstream business press demonstrated the strength of combining traditional and social media tools for the social product manager.

Regardless of the other functional areas impacted, the biggest benefit of social business for the product manager is for themselves. Social business provides a way to float ideas, validate assumptions, test theories, reach a broader audience, or challenge the competition. Sometimes, it does all of the above.

The Social Product Manager's Direct Feedback Loop

In early 2011, I took over a new area of responsibility within the IBM software product line. Until 2011, my main focus had been system administrators, architects, and end users. For the first time, application development tools and developers were part of my focus. Within a few weeks of taking over this new area, I had some ideas about what we could do to grow this business, where we primarily sell an application server software product. However, time was short, and there was no ability to conduct extensive market research.

For both internal IBM and external marketplace audiences, I took to the blogs. On March 7, 2011, I wrote a blog entry titled, "[I]s the ISV [independent software vendor] or the corporate developer a bigger priority?" By asking the question as a binary either/or, I was sure to elicit strong, straightforward opinions from interested readers. No third option was available, and no room was left for "none of the above" answers. To keep the discussion going, I committed to respond to key ideas as they surfaced, across multiple social networking tools.

On edbrill.com, more than 50 responses were received. Via Twitter, email, and internal channels, I received another 50 inputs. The overwhelming answer was that the ISV market was the more important one for me to pursue, and that corporate developers would follow if they saw more ISVs building using the application development tool in question. Almost every response was lengthy, well thought-out, and logical.

Jeremy Hodge, software architect for ZetaOne Solutions Group, wrote:

> *Focus on the ISV, and foster cool exciting new uses of the technology, then that mind share benefits the corporate developer. It's like they say, there is a little bit of a Corvette in every Chevy sold.*[6]

Within a few weeks, my team took forward a proposal internally to introduce a new application server product, targeted at the ISV market. Initially, senior management reacted negatively to the idea, believing that our energy could be better spent on other aspects of the product line. However, once presented with the input from various social channels, the opportunity for introducing the new server became a lot more obvious.

Over the next six months, we prepared a formal business case, came up with a new brand name, devised a new business model for selling the product, and released IBM XWork Server. The incremental investment to devise a new solution for the ISV market was low, making for profitable revenue in an untapped market segment.

IBM XWork Server was designed to sell collaborative applications into organizations with no other existing investment in IBM's collaboration software portfolio. It took the heritage of nearly two decades of Lotus Notes technology and repositioned it into a new market.

XWork Server was an immediate hit. The new product announcement, which I blogged on October 2, 2011, garnered more than 100 comments, 80 Facebook likes, and hundreds of tweets. I made sure to acknowledge the inspiration for the product: "IBM XWork Server is the new product offering *you* built."

The social product manager is not an army of one. The very idea of using social business tools is to enlist the right expertise, knowledge, or innovation at the right time in the product lifecycle. The use of tools and technology results in an ideal intersection of culture and adaptation. The product manager must be supported by an organization and its policies to encourage the risk taking and transparency necessary for success in social business. The payback can be quick, clear, and significant, but the product manager must take the first step: opting in.

Lessons Learned

- The social product manager utilizes direct interaction as a source of input to marketplace understanding, requirements, and decision making.

- The social product manager can create new opportunities simply by having conversations about ideas.

- Social business is about more than technology, it is about cultural change. The social product manager can only be successful in an organization that has become a social business.

- Transparency and truth are important tools for the social product manager. They earn credibility and support more strongly than spin or market-speak.

Endnotes

1. *Wired Magazine,* "The A/B Test: Inside the Technology That's Changing the Rules of Business," Brian Christian, April 2012.

2. Ross Mayfield, "Analysis, Discourse and Influence," August 1, 2004. (http://ross.typepad.com/blog/2004/08/analysis_discou.html). Used with permission.

3. *We the Media: Grassroots Journalism By the People, For the People* by Dan Gillmor. Copyright: 2006, 2004 Dan Gillmor. All rights reserved. Used with permission from O'Reilly Media, Inc.

4. *Forbes,* "Attack of the Blogs," Daniel Lyons, November 2005 (http://tinyurl.com/68j5ry).

5. YouTube, "Why I'm an IBMer," March 2009 (http://tinyurl.com/dzycxu).

6. Jeremy Hodge, comment on EdBrill.com, "With XPages, is the ISV or the corporate developer a bigger priority?" March 7, 2011. Used with permission.

3

Self, Product, or Company

A candid admission: I did it for the ego.

When I first discovered online communities in the context of my work, my participation was motivated by recognition. I was young, inexperienced, and looking to make myself indispensable. As mentioned in the preceding chapter, I also had a strong sense of the truth; perhaps in this context it could be described as self-righteousness or bluster.

The need to feed my ego has long since dissipated, but it leads to the central topic of this chapter: Is the social product manager acting individually, as a product advocate, as a company spokesperson, or as a combination of all of these? Answer: The combination makes for a successful social product manager.

My first job in information technology (IT) was a summer gig stringing cable for a new campus-wide computer network at Indiana University. Intellectually, it wasn't enough of a challenge for me to be lugging wire and crimping connectors; learning about the architecture and the capabilities of the new network made the job interesting. It also led to two fundamental life changes. First, I decided to pursue a career in IT (foregoing an anticipated career path in retail); and second, I started to participate in online communities.

The university at the time operated one of the hallmarks of 1980s hobbyist computing: the bulletin board system (BBS). The BBS was an online gathering place; it was a virtual community that shared information, discussions, and computer files.

Indiana's BBS had fallen into disrepair long before I started working for the University Computing Services organization. I was an active user of the BBS as a student. Now, with the additional role of employee, I was interested in reviving it. Surprisingly, there were some in the university who were happy to have it atrophy and shut down, feeling like it was a relic. The Internet—which we were deploying campus-wide in all those new cables—would indeed soon displace the need for a dial-up service, but at that moment, the BBS was still relevant, and the community that virtually gathered there was worth continuing to nourish.

Even then, gathering support for something I believed in seemed natural. I asked those who were still participating in the BBS to endorse its ongoing operation, and brought that input to the university leadership. The administrators, as is typical, were not particularly fond of a rabble-rousing student telling them what to do. Yet in the end, the dean of the department granted my request for new equipment for the BBS, and the system continued to operate past my matriculation.

Score one for rabble-rousing.

From then on, participating in online communities became part of every aspect of my life. Advocacy did, too. When I became a rookie product manager in the late 1990s, I quickly sought ways to be part of early online communities for my product. Conveniently, that product, IBM Lotus Notes, was one of the early pioneers of Internet forum capability. Our development organization operated a website called Notes.net, which featured a number of such forums.

It was never in my job description to participate in online communities, and in the early days, not on the radar for our business planning or goals. When I became a product manager, I simply sought out a way to establish my voice, and found it in online forums, and subsequently through blogging, internal communities, Twitter, Facebook, LinkedIn, and other tools.

Initially, I couldn't decide whether that voice was an outlet, supplement, or part of my job. It just felt like communicating in this manner was the right approach to connecting with customers and the marketplace, and it also provided a channel for knowledge and input to my job.

In addition to product management, I have spent a good portion of my IBM career in our sales organization. One of the core principles that sales-people all over the world have learned is to "sell" three things: sell yourself, sell your product, and sell your company. As a social product manager, though, initially I struggled with how much these principles applied to online collaboration. I put them in marketer's terms instead: market myself, market my product, and market my company. A product manager typically neither sells nor markets directly, but the social product manager wears many hats.

When I began engaging with the outside world, marketing myself seemed like an important step toward building credibility. It was also the riskiest proposition. If I spent too much time talking about myself, readers would label me arrogant and interested only in hearing my own voice. If I went too deep on the topic of me, I could risk supplying personal details that could become liabilities during the lifetime of information on the Internet. Even more important, if I made my external voice too personal, I risked being attacked on an individual level as a proxy for my company.

Marketing my product was clearly a motivation for writing and contributing every single day. There were risks here, too, though. The nick-name "Brill the shill" was both convenient rhyme and occasionally accurate. Again, credibility was on the line—if I sounded too much like a cheerleader, those I hoped to reach with my words would filter or ignore me. The focus needed, clearly, to be on what the products did, and let the strengths and capabilities speak for themselves. Over time, this has been one of the most important objectives. Chapter 4, "Offense or Defense," also discusses lessons I have learned about when to play offense versus defense in advocating for my products and solutions.

Marketing my company, IBM, was actually the most difficult challenge for me, and continues to be an area where balance is important. The primary product I am responsible for, Lotus Notes, was first released in late 1989, and then acquired by IBM in 1995. Until 2001, IBM allowed the Lotus software organization to operate as a subsidiary "IBM company." As such, for more than a decade, Notes was sold as a Lotus product, not directly branded or affiliated with the greater IBM. The community I interacted with around this product did not see themselves as IBM customers. In some cases, their organizations were very big IBM clients, but the individuals who worked with this particular software were typically isolated from other interactions with IBM. Part of my mission as a social product manager has thus been to help my customers and community transition to seeing my entire company as relevant and reliable.

Each of these three aspects of building credibility online are hence a whole picture that is greater than the sum of its parts. Self, product, company— each demands a different level of conscious judgment around what to say, when to say it, and how to deliver the message.

What follows is a deeper examination of all three of these.

Painting a Self-Portrait

Both inside and outside the organization, social product managers are constantly selling themselves as a measure of authority. In most organizations, the product or brand manager has limited direct power over the departments and people who have to do the actual work of production, sales, marketing, development, and support. Therefore, influence is a strong unit of currency and building integrity critical to success.

In the era of social business, a route to establishing personal credibility is through digital reputation. That starts with selling, or branding, yourself as an individual in the eyes of people both inside and outside the organization.

The trend toward individual brand was first identified in the late 1990s. In 1997, esteemed business writer Tom Peters described individual brand as follows:

> *Regardless of age, regardless of position, regardless of the business we happen to be in, all of us need to understand the importance of branding. We are CEOs of our own companies: Me Inc. To be in business today, our most important job is to be head marketer for the brand called You.*[1]

Social business has revolutionized the process of building individual brand. The "submit" button on internal and external web pages usually captures more than just actual written content; it collects metadata about the person who made the contribution. Company intranets are often filled with the building blocks to create an understanding of the individual humans who make up that organization, including their expertise, experience, and interests. The public Internet likewise associates postings with Facebook pages, Twitter handles, and LinkedIn profiles.

Job titles are still important to convey who owns and does what, but expertise and profile are additional dimensions in personal branding today.

The good news is that they are usually well within your own control, and the opportunity to define yourself as a brand operates on a very wide spectrum.

Because my early public blogging was purely personal writing, readers learned a lot about me as an individual. When the Coca-Cola Company introduced Diet Coke with Lime, my "be lime" blog entry declared my affinity for premixed carbonated water and chemicals. I longingly wrote about a particular type of Japanese ice cream bar that I had hoped to find somewhere at home in America. Pictures of my daughter, car, or home occasionally filtered into blog content.

In short order, the power of my written words morphed into something else. Because they came from "Ed Brill," the IBM guy writing a blog and contributing to communities, they seemed to have extra weight. Customers started referring to my blog and me, as an authoritative voice when sharing Lotus Notes information, as if I was some kind of word-of-truth within the marketplace that I served.

Within a year of starting my blog, I found myself reacting to what had quickly become some kind of quasi-celebrity status within the community of customers and consultants that were reading and participating on EdBrill.com. This was great for the ego, but I started to feel self-conscious about how my ego was being nourished in public. I wrote a blog entry in 2003, quoting one of the hosts of one of my favorite television programs, *Globe Trekker. Globe Trekker* (which was originally called *Lonely Planet*) is/was a travel program hosted by young single travelers who backpack their way through interesting places. At the show's inception, one of the primary hosts was a woman named Justine Shapiro. On this sense of engagement from those around her, she told the *Washington Post*:

> *I also want to dispel any sense that I am a celebrity. I am a single mom, I live in a one-bedroom apartment, I am neither rich nor poor, and my dream is to continue to make documentary films... So I'm a lot like you but I lucked out and got a great gig.* [2]

It has been important to me to retain that sense of fortune and wonder as a social product manager. In selling myself, I have therefore erred on the side of openness. I share my travel adventures in the hope of inspiring others to venture beyond their boundaries. Personal struggles are sometimes—though not always—in the light of day. Interests and curiosities get discussed more broadly than over the dinner table.

I think the last decade of history proves that by sharing of myself I've created more of an opportunity for trust and openness. As previously mentioned, the interactions of a social product manager take place online and offline. To convey to people that I don't already know—but hope to work with—that I am the type of person they would want to work with, too, I have decided to share.

Some of the details of my life that appeared on my blog or public Twitter feed will surprise you, but I believe they are all part of creating the personal brand "Ed Brill":

- In 2006, I was pickpocketed on my way to a train in Kuala Lumpur, Malaysia. It was only the second time in decades of travel I had encountered any real trouble. I didn't lose much, only a paper ticket for my onward flight, a credit card or two, and a small amount of money, but it could have been a lot worse. The travel wallet they lifted out of my briefcase usually also stored my passport. Thankfully it was in my jacket at the time. So, once I had handled rearranging my onward travel and filing a police report, I used my blog as an outlet for sharing the experience, and perhaps starting to heal. The dozen or so comments I received that night surely helped me shake off the experience.

- On three occasions, I have shared my personal struggles with religion on the pages of EdBrill.com. The most recent, in December 2010, coincided with a visit to Jerusalem, an experience that completely misaligned with what I had hoped for. I started the blog entry with a warning that "intensely personal religious emotions follow." Dozens of comments, likes, and tweets later, a comment from Jake Ochs summed up why it was worth taking the risk: *"Thank you, Ed, for sharing your intensely personal feelings about faith in a forthright and respectful way and thank you, to all who commented, for being equally measured and thoughtful in your responses. I have a newfound respect for all of you."* [3]

- On my 42nd birthday, I publicly confessed what I had until then considered a nerdy scar from my childhood: a love for the British television show *Doctor Who*. Since then, friends and readers have often felt comfortable making *Doctor Who* references in their comments and interactions. It's a clear bonding moment. The same held true for my 40th birthday adventure of piloting an airplane for the first time. All the pilots around me have suddenly found a new topic for us to discuss, and I have had offers to go flying in several places as a result.

- When I first started traveling as an adult, I had a "no chain restaurants" rule. I was public about it, and over the years have added several blog and public postings about additional foodie adventures. My coworkers now send me bacon-themed items, plan customer meetings around trying great restaurants, and ask for recommendations when they visit Chicago. (If you are ever passing through my hometown and need a Windy City restaurant recommendation, hit me up on Twitter. I would hate to imagine you eating at a chain restaurant when we have so much great local food.)

- Perhaps most startlingly, EdBrill.com readers know when my older daughter was conceived. The events of September 11, 2001, have had a significant impact on my life and personal beliefs. I often cite the Latin *carpe diem* (seize the day) when making decisions, feeling like at any moment the course of history could change my opportunities in the future. As such, each year I have struggled with whether to acknowledge the anniversary of those events. One year, I wrote about clients I had personally met who perished in the attacks. Another year, I wrote about the contrasts of life around the world. In 2008, though, my then 6-year-old daughter had watched some of the television coverage of the attacks for the first time. When blogging about the anniversary that day, I shared with readers what I shared with my daughter: "My daughter was born in June 2002. This morning, in addition to talking about what happened on 9/11, I told her, 'It was a sad day, but one good thing came out of it: you.'" Was this worth the potential risks to my personal brand? Yes, because as reader Pete B indicated, "I have been missing the personal side of your blog. Seems to have been all business lately. I don't know how other readers feel, but I like the personal touch mixed with business."

"Selling" yourself obviously is a measure of degrees personal decision. Some will feel they are giving up too much of their personal life. Some will feel there is no such thing as a personal life anymore.

The ego that I confessed at the start of this chapter has long since passed. I no longer crave the attention; in fact, at times it's comforting now to avoid having to play my very public role. Getting past "Ed Brill" as a character and into the real me with so many people all over the world has been a wonderful experience. The emails, handshakes, dinner invitations, and friendships have made offering some of my personal self up online worthwhile. But there is a business side, too.

In my business, these offline interactions are what I used as evidence every time someone asked me to help quantify the return on investment from being a social product manager. In the course of an average week, I receive two or three emails from customers or business partners asking for my involvement in a prospective opportunity or customer situation. Their correspondence often starts with an expression of hope such that as I have made myself available online, perhaps I can help with their particular request or opportunity as well. Usually, the answer is yes, or at least I'll try to redirect the request to the right place.

GETTING THINGS DONE

You might be wondering how I have the time to handle all this interaction.

Some days, I am surprised, too.

For a few years, I have used a greatly simplified version of David Allen's *Getting Things Done*® (GTD®) methodology. Allen's bestselling book advocates for a simple method of handling incoming requests:

- Do It.
- Delegate It.
- Defer It.
- Drop It.

I was first exposed to the GTD approach at a seminar conducted by Eric Mack, the author of a software product called eProductivity. The simple principles of GTD have enabled me to become more responsive and helpful, which in turn has led to improved communication, more business opportunities, and increased customer satisfaction. I recommend all of David Allen's books as tools to help the social product manager move from being reactive to proactive about time management and responsiveness.

Positioning Product

Clearly, product or brand managers spends most of their time and energy on their product or service. Any element of positioning that solution in the context of self or company can succeed only if the product is interesting, relevant, and performs as advertised.

The social product manager recognizes that they are the *unique voice* of their product or service. Although other job functions within the organization may utilize the tools of social business to make the product successful, only the product manager can speak with authority and original insight.

Unique voice is a powerful concept in social business. It is like holding the trump card in a poker game. When product managers speak, they carry the weight and credibility of being the source, exclusive insight, and final answer. In the world of social business, all of those capabilities are amplified, with the tools providing both bullhorn and jet rocket for volume and distance of message respectively, both inside a company and to the market at large.

At the same time, unique voice is also the largest inhibitor to product management participation in social business. Product managers cannot brush away their written statements as sales puffery. Product managers risk setting, or mis-setting, customer or market expectations just through the parsing of their words, premature disclosure, or unintended inaccuracy. Forward-looking statements regarding capabilities, pricing, availability dates, or distribution plans can all carry significant financial or legal consequences. The potential land mines are enough to inhibit most product managers, making them feel comfortable only talking about products and services that are available today, rather than futures. Chapter 10, "Risk Management in Social Business," explores some of these challenges further.

Even sticking to today's products and services might not suffice to make a social product manager useful and relevant. An additional challenge in utilizing unique voice successfully is *authenticity*. Social product managers may be tempted to assume a marketing-like tone of positivity online, where their product is the best, great, wonderful solution to any problem ever conceived. However, credibility is built in many ways. Going back to engaged, transparency, and agility, the transparency of a social business is earned through the honesty of interaction. In other words, a social product manager has finally earned the right to say something other than yes.

One Saturday in November 2005, I wrote a blog entry titled "I can't install my own product." [4] I had recently purchased a shiny new Apple iMac for use at home. Primarily, the purchase was influenced by the miracle 30 minutes my then 3-year-old daughter had spent in front of the iMac at the Apple store a few days earlier, the longest attention span I had ever seen her have for anything at that age. Despite insisting to myself that the new computer was going to be a work-free zone, after a few days passed I decided to install the latest version of Lotus Notes on the iMac.

It didn't work.

I struggled with some very basic issues that any customer in the same shoes would have encountered. Certainly, I could have waited until Monday morning and enlisted help from my colleagues. However, I thought that a public blog posting would accomplish two things: I would find out how to address the problem from others who had already encountered and addressed it, and also I would acknowledge a problem to the world at large, building some credibility through transparency and unique voice.

Both worked. By the third comment, someone had helped me address the problem in the short term. By Monday morning, my somewhat-embarrassed development team had added work items to their future plan to try to make the installation of the product on the Mac OS easier. That turned out to be very important, because business usage of Apple Mac computers rocketed exponentially in the subsequent years. With an "it just works" tag line, it was important that IBM's software running on the Mac adopted that mindset as well. The result has been a tremendously positive one, turning a secondary investment into a primary one for IBM, just in time for widespread market adoption of that version of the product.

This particular episode was a carefully calculated risk. Few product development organizations appreciate having their dirty laundry aired in public. In the ensuing years, I rarely have exposed internal issues or debates to the external world, though I have certainly utilized internal social business tools to conduct and extend discussion.

Public visibility into what we sometimes refer to as "sausage making"— the not-necessarily attractive bits of grinding out a product or solution—can sometimes take transparency too far. It may also create discomfort among colleagues and contributors who may feel pressured by spectators or outside opinions. An important lesson here is recognizing when it is acceptable to be open, and anticipate potential consequences.

Sometimes, transparency and agility can be utilized to help address a time-sensitive issue, though they may not solve it. Here the challenge with making statements about the future surfaces in trying to address a problem of the day. In the past, a well-placed "no comment" was sufficient to let a newsworthy issue pass with minimal consequences. In today's social marketplace, though, a head-in-the-sand approach never works.

On June 9, 2008, Apple unveiled the second release of the operating system for the iPhone, where Apple and Microsoft touted integration between the iPhone and Microsoft's Exchange mail server. Every single iPhone would have the ability to use Exchange for email and calendar services, starting with an update coming later in 2008. IBM's equivalent Lotus Notes product was nowhere to be found in the announcement, leaving our customers wondering—often publicly—why we were left behind and whether we would ever provide similar support. Reporters and competitors started to notice the absence of an equivalent capability for IBM customers.

Late that day, I saddled up to my blog a bit defensively and posted an entry titled "iPhone, yes I know!"[5] There were no answers to the hue and cry in my posting, only an acknowledgment of the strong demand and the omission of any answer for future IBM and iPhone customers. I encouraged readers to share their interest in an IBM solution with Apple directly, knowing that like most vendors, Apple reacted more favorably to hearing from customers or prospects than vendors.

The post received more than 100 comments in 48 hours. A petition online received over 400 signatures in a month. A few hundred signatures might not seem that significant, given that now Apple sells half a million iPhones a day. However, the blog post planted an important seed in the public eye, through unique, authentic voice, which eventually grew and blossomed. The seed was the notion that this wasn't solely an IBM decision, as I wrote: "Apple needs to hear it from you. It's much more credible and urgent coming from an Apple customer who wants to buy hundreds of devices...." Within moments, the marketplace knew there was more to the story than could be said publicly and how those who felt strongly about the issue could take action.

Perhaps social business tools weren't going to win the battle that day, but they diffused a negative story for IBM and kicked off an eight-month process that resulted, eventually, in an announcement of support for Lotus Notes on the iPhone in January 2009. That support shipped in October 2009. To a degree, IBM lost a market window of 16 months, but the ongoing public communication about the challenge, plans, beta test release, and eventual shipment of the support meant that our customers could make plans accordingly. By the time the iPhone was ready for mainstream business adoption,

IBM was ready for the iPhone. Social business—not just the use of social media tools but the actual engagement, transparency, and agility of both IBM and our customers and business partners—had succeeded, taking advantage of a highly visible situation and turning it into one where IBM could continuously engage with all parties toward a solution.

Those two last examples were somewhat negative, and in Chapter 4 I examine the opportunities to play offense versus defense for the social product manager. Selling your product online often draws on a bit of both tactics, while other times, you aren't playing a game at all.

For IBM, one of the most successful tools we have used for engaging our customers, partners, and employees, is known as an online jam. A jam is a focused, short-duration set of structured discussions around ideas and opportunities. IBM's first public jam was an innovation jam in 2008. The jam benefited from nearly 90,000 logins that generated more than 32,000 posts. It tapped employees from more than 1,000 companies across 20 industries— including thousands of IBMers, as well as independent authorities from a variety of fields. Several of these independent authorities also played lead roles in guiding Jam discussions, such as subject matter experts from Mars Incorporated, Eli Lilly and Company, Citigroup, and the Boston College Center for Corporate Citizenship.

Ideation is a social product management discipline that has grown out of the jam concept. It takes the old concept of the suggestion box mixed with the social business tool of crowdsourcing. Bring together like-minded individuals, and they can come up with more ideas faster and more in line with the market than traditional methods of research and development. Ideation is now practiced by organizations in many different industries globally:

- Starbucks coffee hosts an ideation website at MyStarbucksIdea.com. MyStarbucksIdea allows coffeehouse aficionados to share their best ideas for improving Starbucks. Two years after launch, more than 80,000 ideas had been submitted. Starbucks has credited the site with over 50 improvements to their business in the first two years. Not all of the ideas from the site were brand new to their product managers, nor were all of them improvements in actual Starbucks products, but the site is clearly a success and a critical marketing tool.[6]

- In 2010, the U.S. Department of the Interior launched a website called America's Great Outdoors, following the announcement of an initiative by President Barack Obama in April 2010. One of the features of the website was a jam, based on Elguji's Ideajam, which runs on IBM software. During the America's Great Outdoors jam, nearly 500,000 votes were cast for potential U.S. Department of Interior projects. More than 2,000 ideas were submitted and consider by the American government as potential expansion or improvement at national parks and recreational areas.

■ CEMEX, a global building materials provider, adopted ideation as part of an internal project called Shift. Shift won Forrester Research's 2010 Groundswell Award for management collaboration system. According to CEMEX, "A large number of new ideas are now having exposure and transparency in Shift. Ideas not only come from top management but from employees at every organizational level. Positive feedback is received to find areas of opportunity, as well as negative feedback to find ways to improve the collaboration among employees. Since Shift's launch, a few idea jam sessions have taken place where hundreds of employees have posted their proposals for consideration. At the same time, a series of Global Innovation Initiatives, teams that seek new ways to reach global strategic goals, were established. The progress of these initiatives has been closely followed up by all Shift users, as they are setting the pace for innovation through collaboration. Their value lies not only in the new solutions they may find to their challenges, but also in proving the value of collaboration through Shift."[7] Shift is not an example of direct product management-related ideation, but it demonstrates how internal audiences can utilize social business tools to identify new opportunities for innovation and speed to market. The best ideas for how an organization can improve can come from anywhere: sales, marketing, product development, even finance or human resources. CEMEX reaches internally for one source of input into the overall product development cycle, and has found new ideas and improvements through this engagement model.

IDEATION: THE PRODUCT MANAGER'S NEW BEST FRIEND

A popular social business trend the past couple of years has been the concept of ideation: the process of generating new ideas in an online community. Participants provide ideas in response to a series of "challenge questions" asked by a product manager, chief innovation officer, or the executive team.

Ideation is an amazing way to collect the voices of your customers and constituents in order to get feedback on products, processes, and services. Once collected, ideas can be voted on and discussed by all members of the community. Popular ideas bubble to the top, and it's not uncommon to see less-feasible ideas get voted down. When this happens, an active community typically discusses why the idea may not be a good one.

Companies such as IBM, the U.S. Department of Agriculture, and Starbucks have successfully used public ideation communities to connect with their customers and deliver new products and services. In addition to public uses of ideation software, many companies have crowdsourced new ideas from within the company.

Product managers at Starbucks had to have been thrilled when one of their customers submitted an idea for the now-infamous green "splash stick" on the My Starbucks Idea site. Prior to the splash stick, baristas would put white tape over the coffee lid to prevent coffee from spilling, a less than ideal solution because customers did not appreciate the leftover residue on the coffee lid. Now, a tiny green "splash stick" fits perfectly into the coffee lid and pops into place. No mess and happy commuting customers.

During the economic downturn of 2009, American President Barack Obama challenged all U.S. government employees to make cost-saving suggestions for the annual U.S. budget process through an online idea jam. This was part of a larger effort to ensure that the U.S. government agencies invested taxpayer dollars in programs and initiatives that have proven records of success and either fix or end programs that do not.

To meet the challenge, the Department of Agriculture used an ideation software tool called IdeaJam created by IBM Business Partner Elguji Software, Inc., to connect with their 105,000 employees and collect their ideas, votes, and discussions. The department used the collective intelligence of their employees to help make the hard cost-cutting decisions that needed to be made.

When product managers at IBM wanted to get feedback on a new marketing initiative, they used Elguji's IdeaJam ideation platform to facilitate a three-day public Lotus Knows IdeaJam. In only three days, 947 ideas were submitted by end users, business partners, and software developers. The jam generated 20,449 votes and 2,246 comments. The data was then presented to IBM in a concise series of reports that they used to analyze the results of the jam.

Ideation tools have become a core component in many social software platforms, including IBM's Connections product. Each community within Connections can now include an ideation blog that can be used to share, comment, and vote on ideas. Ideas can then be turned into Connections activities, helping community managers track the progress of an idea through the innovation process.

The voice of the customer has never been more important, and product managers have incredible tools available to easily capture and engage with new ideas. For businesses and organizations that make it easy for customers to provide feedback and interact seamlessly with organization-wide ideation practices, they will be more competitive and responsive to the immediate needs and wants of the digital world.

—Bruce Elgort, president and CEO, Elguji Software

Representing the Company

Social business tools provide a significant opportunity for organizations to establish and strengthen their brand and products, reaching a much broader audience with more content than ever before. Each of the individual participating voices shapes the perception of the company.

Part of the culture of participation must establish that individuals represent the company responsibly and authentically. As described in earlier chapters, our philosophy at IBM has been to encourage individual voices to represent IBM's assets across all the markets, industries, and geographies where we operate. This effort has dramatically changed how IBM is perceived in the marketplace, such that the IBM brand is now the second-most-valuable brand, according to the 2012 BrandZ Top 100.[8]

The challenge for many organizations, ours included, is that individual employees often feel like they cannot represent the company at large, yet from an outside point of view they are expected to do so. Readers see the title and employer of a contributor to a website, blog, online discussion, tweet, or LinkedIn or Facebook group, and instantly ascribe that comment to the person's job responsibility and their employer.

At IBM, we have provided a bit of a safety net by encouraging employees to use a standard disclaimer that their social content is "not necessarily represent[ing] IBM's positions, strategies, or opinions." Still, when I or others speak, we appear to be the voice of the company. Plus, as I have moved up in the organization, and concurrently the use of social tools has broadened, it has definitely impacted the way in which I communicate.

Positioning IBM on social networks meant getting comfortable with being part of IBM in the first place. From college onward, it had been my dream to work for IBM. Yet when my then-employer, Lotus Development, was acquired by IBM in 1995, it took years for us individually and collectively to truly assimilate and operate like part of IBM. This was by design, as Lotus Notes and the other Lotus brand products were essentially the first end-user software IBM had ever acquired. Management believed that the transition, if it ever took place, needed to be gradual. Existing Lotus customers perceived Big Blue as an element of risk to a great product and ecosystem. Over time, the strength of the IBM brand and commitment to the product has been a critical success factor, but one that I and others have had to "sell" to customers who had a historical affinity with Lotus. Of course, external social media has been a key tool for that transition; a frequent theme on my blog is the storyline "IBM is good for Lotus Notes."

For IBM, like many companies, another challenge is the portfolio nature of our business. IBM has a broad vision and operates in a number of businesses. It is quite common, as it is for many such organizations, for employees in one part of the business—for example, software—to have little knowledge of the details of another part of the business, such as consulting services. The same is true for customers; the particular product they use might have little or no connection to other parts of the IBM family, especially acquired solutions.

My particular products went through the evolution to be fully part of IBM in a very prolonged way. Even 16 years after acquisition by IBM, customers and business partners found the branding of IBM Lotus Notes confusing. Because customers often associated "Lotus" with 1-2-3®, the first mainstream desktop spreadsheet, or earlier versions of Lotus Notes, the brand wasn't always a positive attribute.

In anticipation of an eventual transition to utilizing only the IBM brand, and moving Notes to simply a product name, I wrote a blog entry in July 2011 titled "Whatever we call it":

{W}e've come to the realization on some products... that to get into new customers, the Lotus brand sometimes brings history, sometimes challenging history, and thus, rather than try to force the brand to fit into places where it isn't a best foot forward, it makes more sense to use the 2nd most-valuable brand in the world, IBM.

This post garnered nearly 100 comments, 75 tweets, and 50+ Facebook likes. Among the comments was Tim Tripcony: "I agree that marketing is important, but I couldn't care less what the product is called as long as it meets our customers' needs... it does, and will continue to." [9]

However, the blog post was controversial inside of IBM. As a product manager, I had taken it upon myself to communicate externally about branding, clearly a marketing function in our organization. I had stepped on toes, forcefully. Part of the challenge of selling your company through social networking is recognizing the occasions where the organization's voices are disconnected and the effort needed to unite those voices.

Part of my goal in writing the blog entry was to promote other IBM voices on the topic of branding. Lending my own digital reputation to colleagues confers credibility and respect to those other individuals. At least 10 percent of all my blog entries on EdBrill.com are links to other IBMers and their content. I also occasionally feature "guest blog" entries from colleagues. The more unique voices that can be brought to the conversation, credibly, the louder and clearer the message.

Today, in recognition of how important reputation is to a company as well as its individuals, IBM has adopted a Digital IBMer initiative to showcase how every single employee contributes making IBM the best-in-class example of a social business. Across product groups, divisions, and countries, all IBMers globally are embracing the internal and external use of social business tools.

The Digital IBMer effort has support at every single level of the organization. The goals, as conveyed to all our employees, are "to focus IBM interactions on concrete outcomes that deliver business value: enhancing social presence, increasing and projecting expertise, engaging with clients, and collaborating to innovate." A Digital IBMer hub has been deployed on our company intranet, with education and employee enablement tools.

This isn't just talk. In March 2012, IBM CEO Ginni Rometty visited IBM's Chicago office and conducted a town hall meeting, which I attended.

Yet among the hundreds of colleagues in the room that day, I felt like she was speaking directly to me in her discussion of the Digital IBMer.

Rometty indicated that she thought it was critical for IBM not only be the market-leading provider of social business tools but also that we as an organization must demonstrate to the market how we are living proof of the success of social business.

I certainly felt like my team and I were part of that living proof. However, it seems unlikely that Rometty knew that a few weeks earlier IBM Press had approached me to write a book on social business from a product/brand management point of view. Initially, I had been skeptical about undertaking such a project.

Listening to Rometty, the company's leader, describing the importance of confirming IBM's success as a social business, my attitude quickly changed. It became clear that the most important individual contribution I could make to the initiative was to embrace a decade of success and tell the world about it. That day, *Opting In* was born.

Success in selling yourself and your product depends on others in your organization also being social. Each of you represents the company with your own unique voice, but with varying audiences and reputations.

When I joined the company in 1994, I had never been in a sales organization. A few months into the job, I attended my first sales meeting. The theme of the meeting—I remember thinking it was crazy to have an actual slogan just for a meeting—was "One vision, many voices." We also used a tagline for years of "Working together." Put these two thoughts together and they will guide how to sell yourself, your product, and your company as a social product manager.

Lessons Learned

- Self, product, and company are the three dimensions of individual success in social business, and the social product manager must be cognizant of all three.
- Personal branding establishes leadership, expertise, authenticity, and credibility, while demonstrating willingness to take risks.
- Social product managers contribute their *unique voice* in social business, with the authority of being the subject matter expert and not simply amplification.

■ The voice and presence of social product managers represent not just themselves or their product but also their company in the external market. This might stretch the product management job description, but company advocacy, or promotion of other company voices, can be used to add to credibility and reputation.

Endnotes

[1] Tom Peters, *Fast Company* magazine, "The Brand Called You," August 31, 1997 (www.fastcompany.com/28905/brand-called-you).

[2] Justine Shapiro, *Washington Post,* "'Globe Trekker': South Africa," May 22, 2003 (http://tinyurl.com/8lq9rag).

[3] Jake Ochs, comment on EdBrill.com "Jerusalem," December 6, 2010 (www.edbrill.com/ebrill/edbrill.nsf/dx/jerusalem). Used with permission.

[4] Blog entry on EdBrill.com, "I can't install my own product" (www.edbrill.com/ebrill/edbrill.nsf/dx/i-cant-install-my-own-product).

[5] Blog entry on EdBrill.com, "Redirect iPhone > /yes/i/know" (www.edbrill.com/ebrill/edbrill.nsf/dx/redirect-iphone-yesiknow).

[6] From *Brand Autopsy* by John Moore, "Tough Love for Starbucks," January 26, 2010 (http://tinyurl.com/8h4nyyv).

[7] CEMEX website (www.cemex.com/whatisshift/cxshift_innovation.htm).

[8] 2012 BrandZ Top 100 from Millward Brown (www.millwardbrown.com/BrandZ/Top_100_Global_Brands.aspx).

[9] Tim Tripcony, comment #26 on EdBrill.com, "Whatever We Call It," July 2, 2011 (www.edbrill.com/ebrill/edbrill.nsf/dx/whatever-we-call-it).

4

Offense or Defense

Product management is a sport. You might never have thought of product or brand management in the context of sport, but every one of us plays both offense and defense on a daily basis.

The social product manager is the player/coach who has the opportunity to take charge and drive initiatives, as well as withstand and resist attack. Both offense and defense can be used to overcome obstacles, reset expectations, and focus individuals and teams on achieving results.

This chapter explores the notion of when a social product manager should use which set of tactics. Importantly, we examine these techniques through the lenses of engaged, transparent, and nimble as discussed earlier, as well as the importance of credibility and unique voice, as discussed in Chapter 3, "Self, Product, or Company."

Tactical analysis in social business has four key steps:

1. **Perform a situation analysis.** First, is the need to create a positive and proactive message about something being invented, announced, done, recognized, or celebrated? Conversely, is the aim to disseminate factual information designed to respond to others such as customers, competitors, reporters, or analysts?

2. **Determine timing.** Does the topic at hand need to be addressed immediately, or is pacing or progressive disclosure important? Is the information timed to some other activity such as a press release or product announcement, is it tied into a discussion already taking place, or is it making news on its own?

3. **Establish volume and amplification.** Where will this message be communicated? Internally, externally, or both? Using what vehicles—blog, public social networks, internal social networks, sharing sites, or some combination? Chapter 6, "Activate Your Advocates," explores the specific kinds of tools the social product manager can use for external communication, but this chapter builds to the decision point of why and when to utilize them.

4. **Anticipate unintended consequences.** The fourth and final step is to play out the chess board, preparing for what will happen when the social product manager speaks with a unique, authentic voice. What could be the unforeseen consequences? In the chess game, was the offensive move toward checkmate, or did we only manage to protect the queen?

Situation Analysis

One of my best lessons learned over the years is that most communication should be positive. It is surprising how often that isn't the case.

I work for a successful company and own a successful product, one that has been number one or number two in its market for more than 20 years. Most of what I want to talk about with my customers, partners, and colleagues is good news—new products, new features, successful adoption, competitive differentiation, recognition.

Often I am asked, "How do you know what information to blog/tweet/share?" Inspiration for good, useful outbound communication comes from many places.

For example, a customer meeting, where a specific product capability was discussed, can prompt introspection on whether other customers might want to know more about that capability. An internal debate, discussing how to approach a problem or opportunity, may lead to questions that are best answered through direct market interaction. An article or email I read may spur the thought that other voices may have something to contribute on the same topic. A timely piece of news may need visibility or is timed with a broader announcement. A news story or analyst report may need a reaction, or nonreaction, from the vendor to round out the picture.

Consider this example: A message to the marketplace is multipurpose, as in the simple example of a screenshot that I posted on EdBrill.com in May 2012, as shown in Figure 4.1. The image was of the then-upcoming version of Lotus Notes, called Social Edition. I provided no written commentary, just the picture of an email inbox in the planned new version of Lotus Notes.

Figure 4.1   EdBrill.com: Lotus Notes Social Edition preview, May 2012.

What prompted me to share that screenshot that day? In small part, simply because it was ready for me to share it externally. I had seen it myself just a few days earlier, and thought the then-current iteration looked strong enough to make a public debut.

However, there were many additional motivations. This was primarily an offensive move. I wanted customers and prospects to see the real work that was going on in our engineering organization to transform the product visually. That particular effort, designed to modernize the user interface, had started with a blueprint more than two years earlier. It was exciting to finally be in a position to show the world an early look at the results. I also wanted to start to build some awareness that the new version was progressing and that we would begin to talk about it more publicly. Further, I wanted our engineering team to receive some feedback and recognition that they were on the right path with the new interface, which would hopefully provide encouragement as well as satisfaction with what had been accomplished so far.

On defense, there were yet more reasons that I thought the timing was appropriate to post the screenshot. This new release of Lotus Notes was designed to improve our footing competitively. Showing the new Lotus Notes might reduce pressure from end users who expressed a preference to use products from other vendors. That pressure traditionally strengthened in May and June of each year, as Microsoft—our primary competitor—operated on a July to June fiscal year. I believed that if I could show my own customers that we were making the right product improvements they would be less interested in considering alternatives.

The blog entry received over 50 comments, another 50 tweets, 40 Facebook "likes," and it generated secondary discussion on other blogs and public social streams. Some of the comments wanted more such images, or advocated for other potential product enhancements, but by and large, the response to the screenshot was positive. Some were quite enthusiastic, including Christian Tillman's: "How can I bribe you to get my hands on this NOW?"

An interesting secondary effect was created with this posting, however. When IBM announced the new Lotus Notes Social Edition, some customers were confused by the name because it lacked a version number for identification. The blog entry, with only a screenshot, received several comments on how the new product name had multiple potential interpretations. Inside of IBM, we were hearing that feedback as well. These social interactions, not the result of formal market research, served as early indication that adjustment to the product naming might be necessary.

A few weeks later, my team reevaluated the product name for this new release, bringing in the version number 9.0. Marketing-wise, our direction continued to emphasize the new product name, but for the sake of continuity and familiarity, we accepted and fine-tuned based on market feedback in real time. I considered it a fortunate unintended consequence of the posting, because it gave us the opportunity to make changes before the product was actually released.

The situation analysis is thus critical for the social product manager. Because the product manager speaks with unique, authentic voice, every communication must be weighed carefully. Product managers are often jokingly derided for the typical response to customer feedback: "Thanks for that input, we'll take it into consideration." That phrase appears on millions of web pages, because it is a true statement that makes no commitment. Because of timing and amplification, the visibility of a social interaction carries higher risks of setting—or mis-setting—expectations, thus sometimes it seems like it is just easier to make no comment. I want to encourage you to take the risk.

Here are some suggestions for ways to start a conversation... on offense:

- **Functional details that provide additional data about a current or future product.** This includes capabilities you take for granted, but your readers may not.

- **A customer success story, even if you can't name the client.** Social media readers accept the notion that not every customer wants their name used as a reference. Readers attribute the information to the writer and rely on the trust established between the writer and their client.

- **Insight into how a particular product decision was made.** A way to build credibility and deepen your relationship with readers is to share the back story behind choices and decisions.

- **Great moments in history that are relevant today.** Sometimes these are opportunities to celebrate past decisions or milestones, other times they might be a chance to use the past as a predictor of future success.

Here are some suggestions for ways to start a conversation... on defense:

- **Point of view on timely news items.** The next section covers timing in more detail. Don't shy away from potentially negative or even controversial topics. A well-reasoned question or opinion can be better than saying nothing.

- **Situations that need improvement.** So long as you don't sound apologetic, an opportunity-driven conversation about a gap or miss is just fine.

- **A missed opportunity.** These require some caution because you do not want to frequently criticize your own decision making. However, self-criticism—which utilizes authentic voice—might provide feedback on how to do things better the next time.

Timing

The old cliché "timing is everything" applies in spades to the social product manager. Product managers have always had to consider product launch plans, competitor actions, industry reports, conferences and events, and other factors when timing communications. The era of social business, along with real-time access to information through mobile devices, is further compressing cycle time. The social product manager must now weigh the axis of immediacy in determining when to communicate.

On offense, time is a lot easier to control. In the era of social business, product management still needs to tie into product lifecycle management and marketing execution. However, it does introduce a new requirement for preparedness.

Today, announcing a new product at an event virtually guarantees that someone *other* than the person/company making the announcement will be the first to talk about it online. As-it-happens use of social media has inspired a whole culture of advocates and reporters who will jump at any opportunity to provide a first reaction to "news" of any variety. The moment the word is out, the message conveyed—whether accurate or not—takes on a life of its own.

The social product manager can use this to their advantage. *Progressive disclosure* is an effective construct to apply to the timing of commentary regarding current, planned, or future products. Rather than release news all at once, I use social media to build awareness, interest, and "buzz" leading up to the actual communication of news. This primes the audience to expect something specific, makes them aware that there will in fact be something to pay attention to, and most important, it allows me to retain some sense of authentic voice and original ownership of the news as it happens.

Historically, my division within IBM has taken advantage of an annual conference—held in Orlando, Florida, for nearly two decades—as a key location to introduce new products. The conference itself is a model of predictability; thousands of customers come to the event every year precisely because of its familiarity. The conference attendees have been trained that our big announcements for the event will be in the opening session, which always occurs on Monday morning.

For the past several years, I've taken a seat in the audience during that opening session and operated a sort of social media hub in real time. I prewrite blog entries on the topics of our major announcements, and then capture the crowd reactions in the room itself right before pressing the Publish button. Simultaneously, I monitor Twitter and live blogs for the sentiment of those both at the conference and watching from afar. The real-time presence allows me to share first-person perspectives with all the online interested parties—keeping the vendor's voice in the conversation. My blog entries often become quote material for reporters covering the event from afar, because they, too, have learned over the years to check for my content coming out of the conference's opening session.

During the first few hours of the conference, my goal is to capture the real-time buzz and use social media to foreshadow additional news and provide tips to other worthwhile sessions for those attending the conference.

One other useful plan for a conference or event is to have preplanned content themes for the subsequent days of the event and use blogging as a summary and wrap-up vehicle when it is all over. Chapter 6 further examines how to engage the audience at an event from a product manager's point of view.

Choreography is not inconsistent with unique, authentic voice. As long as the social product manager uses an engagement model that is transparent, and presents a dialogue rather than a monologue, the coordinated, precise timing of an activity on offense will be accepted and generate further discussion and goodwill. Further, the original information will often be quickly amplified as the initial wave of reactions continues and those seeking the news of the day elect to also pass it along.

Timing is also relevant when playing defense. Social business tools give product managers the opportunity to engage directly in fighting fires and negativity. To extend the metaphor, the question then becomes this: Is the product manager a first responder, a relief valve, or consciously avoiding getting involved in a situation? The answer could be any of these, depending on a situation.

Crisis management is still a discipline best left to the communications professionals in your organization; when a corporation needs to stay on message, unique voice is not an option. However, there might be smaller-scale negative situations where the social product manager is ideally suited to engage in a situation real time. In fact, the social product manager is often the best person to play defense, in situations where more formal or traditional marketing tools would be disproportionate responses.

For example, computer software is an industry segment where predicting the future with any certainty is challenging. Risk-adverse IT organizations often ask for a multiyear roadmap in an industry where the technology life-cycle is short. Five years ago, there were no iPhones or iPads, so a 2008 product strategy statement would likely have ignored smartphones or tablets, both primary interfaces to technology today.

In early October 2011, we released a new version of IBM Lotus Notes and Domino. It was an important release, with the introduction of new products and software bundles in the product line. For a couple of days, my outbound messages were 100 percent focused on the themes of this new release.

The last thing a product manager wants to worry about following a launch is what happens next, but defensively, I ended up having to discuss the future just days after the software was released. It seemed that my competition was waiting for the actual release to unleash a rumor in the market—that this new update was going to be the last release of Lotus Notes ever made by IBM.

The timing of the rumor could not have been worse. IBM had worked hard to deliver an on-time update to our clients, yet in turn had to spend time fielding questions from all over the world about the product's longevity. Responding to such a rumor was risky because the answer could serve as an acknowledgment that there was some basis for the story.

I turned to my blog as a vehicle for reaching the community who had grown to trust me as the voice of authority on all things Lotus Notes. Only two days after a new product release, it was time to publish a blog entry titled "Roadmap for Notes/Domino From Here." The blog was only two paragraphs long. It indicated IBM's plan to continue to ship new releases of Lotus Notes, with a general commitment to two new versions in the coming three years. I was careful not to discuss any specific features or capabilities we intended to add to the product in those releases, simply to reassure readers that there was a future for the product.

The strategy worked: 50 tweets, 50 Facebook likes, and reblogged in German and Italian. The comments were positive, too, including collabora-tion software developer and author Tom Duff:

Nice to see planning 2 to 4 years out, Ed... good post.[1]

I gave one small hint in the opening of the posting that there had been a defensive reason to discuss the future roadmap at that particular time, saying, "Because there is discussion." However I didn't indicate specifically what the catalyst for the blog post had been, which would have fueled the rumor. Instead, I simply shared facts as they existed at that moment, which extin-guished the fire and quelled the rumor.

Timing was critical with that post. Had I allowed the rumor to continue in the market without any acknowledgment from IBM, it would have grown in strength. The volume mattered, too, as a press release or other disproportionate response to the rumor would have only served to give it more attention.

There were several ways to address the rumor. By publishing a blog entry that asserted the future, most never realized there was such a rumor, they only saw a blog post on the future of the product and moved on. A tweet or Facebook post or LinkedIn discussion might not have conveyed the strength of the statement, whereas the blog post was more permanent and was explicitly written both for the timing and also to stand the test of time.

Social product managers do not always have to use social vehicles as part of their communications strategy. The right answer for timing sometimes is never. Part of the situation analysis has to be a decision on whether to engage in a battle or not in the first place. Silence is often useful, especially where the product itself stands to gain nothing from engagement. As a social product manager, though, silence is sometimes deafening, because both external and internal audiences may have developed an expectation of engagement.

Even the title of this book, *Opting In,* is derived from the question of a timing scenario in which the right answer could be never. In social networking, there is often an expectation that a groundswell of volume will draw all interested parties into a discussion. The social product manager must use the situation and analysis, timing, and volume as analytical points to determine when to opt in to playing offense, defense, or sitting on the sidelines.

Volume and Amplification

One of the hard lessons of social business is that not everyone will hear everything said by anyone. While social media tools have provided great empowerment for sharing of information, multiplier effects are still relevant to conveying your message and having it be properly understood.

The notion of reach applies in two dimensions, both outbound and inbound. Outbound, social business tools provide new ways to communicate key messages; and inbound, customers and prospects share information that can drive buying decisions and adoption.

Social media users often have an assumption of perfect reach. Twitter users who "at" vendors or brands—myself included from time to time—believe they are communicating their likes or dislikes to those vendors. Usually, there is a community manager on the receiving end, who may or may not be empowered and trained to route information, find experts, or even provide adequate responses. They might be using sentiment analysis tools to provide pattern-matched input into broad organizational strategy and decisions. Alternatively, there might be little organizational commitment to the social media presence, providing rote responses or ignoring inbound messages completely. Obviously, the company behind the presence may have very different reach and impact depending on their commitment.

Inbound, volume contributes to the situation analysis and catalyzes timing. Outbound, volume increases the likelihood of your message hitting the intended target, but also carries risks of saturation. Volume is a tricky component of message delivery to get right.

The social product manager who is engaged in the market might choose to develop the instinct of a surfer, watching for the right waves to roll and carry him in. A particular topic of interest might surface in the market as the result of a knowledge-sharing blog post or publication of a case study. Should that reflect favorably on your product, it's time to ride the wave and amplify, through a product manager's unique voice.

Volume is such a common concern in social business that I offer both an inbound and an outbound example of lessons learned.

Most product managers recognize that incremental improvement is often as important as introducing new products or new ways of doing business. Sometimes, addressing the little things will garner as much goodwill as the major announcements.

In March 2009, Paul Mooney shared a long-standing frustration. Mooney is a senior technical architect at European consulting firm BlueWave Technology and an influential blogger. Mooney was unhappy that IBM software, as downloaded from our website, was stored in a file using the product's IBM part number as its name. After downloading a product, he couldn't identify it, because the part number meant nothing to him as a human, only to IBM systems.

Mooney's blog entry demanding that IBM "sort out your software downloads"[2] was forthright. The time had come for change. Dozens of IBM customers and other business partners commented on Mooney's site, sometimes in even more ardent terms.

Although somewhat uncomfortable, Mooney's blog provided an opportunity. The words of the customer and market directly could be used to draw attention internally at IBM to this long-standing issue.

Links to Mooney's blog were shared with my team and colleagues. This highlights an important component of social business: Not everyone needs to participate. Those who would then be directed to read Mooney's blog might not ever comment there or even speak to a customer directly, but they now were being social, by consuming information directly from the marketplace.

It turned out, these cryptic filenames could be easily rectified. While perhaps at some point in the past IBM systems had required them, IBMers reading the feedback from Paul Mooney's blog realized they could use descriptive filenames in the same system. There was no reason, except for historical behavior, for Mooney's concern to even exist.

On April 1, 2009, only a few weeks later, I posted on my own blog that the market had been heard, and in the future files downloaded from IBM.com would have identifiable names, not just serial numbers.[3] A blog was the right tool because of both the ability to have public, shared discussion, the permanence of the blog entry, and the ability to recognize Mooney's contribution in the largest possible spotlight. Search engines such as Google would provide a reference point, forever commemorating that this change in how IBM operated was a result of social networking. A one-line announcement on the product download site would never properly explain the change, nor reinforce the dialogue with the market.

Problem solved. Readers reacted immediately, applauding IBM for listening to the market. One blog reader claimed to have cried tears of joy upon learning of the change. It just took a volume of suggestions to reach the right people—within a nimble organization, engaged with the market to make things happen.

DOWNLOADGATE

"Downloadgate" is a good example of IBM embracing the shift of culture to a more open and social world. Relevant people in IBM noticed the crowd sentiment on the blog post and identified many of the commenters as influential in the online community. In the older days, single complaints may have been lost in due process, and crowd frustration would have continued. Now IBM had little choice but to identify the issue and react to it. They did so, in a positive manner.

—Paul Mooney, August, 2012

Sometimes, the amplification is more fine-grained, picking up several smaller voices and bringing them into one message.

Like most products, Lotus Notes is sold in several different packaging options. One type are our Express® offerings, typically sold to small and midsize companies with fewer than 1,000 employees at a discounted price. Express packages were created around 2002, and they differ from our enterprise offerings by restricting some of the functionality of the product. However, some of those restrictions were showing their age in 2010, and a wave of feedback came into IBM from customers, resellers, and solution vendors that it was time for a change.

On offense, my team analyzed the input we received through all those channels and elected to update the packaging for Express. We believed it could increase sales if we made some changes in the name of modernization. We decided to drop the main technical restriction, a feature called clustering that allows customers to deploy two servers as mirror images and provide more reliability.

On November 29, 2010, I wrote a blog entry announcing the planned change coming on January 1, 2011, dubbing it a "holiday present" and wrapping it in a bow. After publishing, it was time to sit back in my chair and wait for the wave of applause to roll in.[4]

Within minutes, six of the first ten comments suggested that perhaps there had been a misunderstanding despite the volume of input received from the market. Very directly, most said some form of "that's nice, but what about these other restrictions?" There were additional differences in the Express products that we had left in place, thinking that there needed to be some technical differentiation to justify the discount to smaller organizations.

Apparently, the market disagreed.

One of the risks of social business, one which I comment further on in Chapter 10, "Risk Management in Social Business," is incomplete distribution. The volume heard through social media, for example, might represent only a subset of the market. In most cases, the subset will represent a relative distribution, but sometimes, there are still blind spots.

With the planned change in our Express offerings, I had clearly had several blind spots. It was so important to make the big impact change that the market had demanded for so long that the chance to get it right the first time actually was missed.

Progressive disclosure would have helped. I had not tested my plans much, internally or externally. Because the volume on this issue had been so loud for so long, it seemed like a classic no-brainer decision. The feedback showed it was, but it was an incomplete one.

What about the scenarios where amplification is desired to take a message far beyond its original recipients? Can the social product manager create a meme, or at least a groundswell? Chapter 6 picks up the amplification theme and discusses ways to carry your message far and wide.

Anticipation and Unintended Consequences

Like our marketing colleagues, product managers need to anticipate market reactions and customer responses to outbound communications. Sharing strategy, direction, positioning, or capabilities never happens in a vacuum, and the traditional game of "telephone" can be quickly amplified—not always for the better—through social business tools.

The Appendix, "IBM Social Computing Guidelines," contains, unsurprisingly, IBM's social computing guidelines. They draw extensively on a mindset of saying and doing the right thing, and I constantly refer to these guidelines in the course of social networking. While planning a blog, tweet, or forum comment, the last and often most important step, though, is applying the front page news test. Does it feel comfortable that what I'm about to say could show up on the landing page or printed first page of a news publication, attributed to Ed Brill, IBM executive? Will that lead to any unanticipated impact in the market, for example, through interpretation by customers or competitors? Am I saying what I mean and meaning what I say?

In other words, *authentic voice* has some limits.

One of the most obvious ones is the competitor spin inhibitor. The social product manager should consider their words in the context of how a competitor might use them, typically out of context.

In February 2012, the CEO of Jive Software, Tony Zingale, told IT publication *Information Week* that IBM Connections, our social software platform product, is the "refurbished Lotus email system."[5] Zingale probably thought he could attempt to tie a newer IBM product to an older one and create uncertainty in readers' minds when they saw that quote. Zingale probably did not anticipate IBM responding, as Vice President of Social Software Jeff Schick did in the comments section of the article:

When I was growing up and people were talking jive, they were talking nonsense. Nonsense that goes unchallenged becomes fact. Tony made the statement that "IBM Connections is the refurbished Lotus email system." This statement is plain jive talk.

Already, though, Schick was walking a fine line between humor and picking a fight. Zingale's credibility had been called into question. Schick, however, went further:

In IDC's marketshare surveys for the last two years on Enterprise Social Software, IBM is #1 and Jive is a distant #3. That is a fact.

In instigating competitor ire, Jive CEO Zingale had actually given his competition a platform to attack him. Worse yet, other competitors piled on, making additional superiority claims over Jive.

All of this might have gone unnoticed but for the fact that Jeff Schick is a social product management executive. He tweeted a link to the article and posted it on his IBM intranet profile, which drew attention from other IBMers and the market at large. Soon, the *Information Week* story was big news, with over 550 shares on Google+.

Perhaps Zingale will apply the front page test next time.

Unintended consequences can also apply to the offense equation, if the social product manager gets caught up in the instantaneousness of social media. Over the past decade, one of my favorite comments on EdBrill.com was this from IBM business partner Mikkel Flindt Heisterberg of Denmark:

As a result of the blogosphere, the distance between me and IBM has never been shorter.[6]

Sometimes, the ability to garner immediate feedback through social business tools is intoxicating. I see informal feedback on product requirements coming through my internal and external social networking all the time. However, getting caught up in the emotion of input can lead to group think and knee-jerk reaction, rather than well thought-out brand management.

Earlier in this chapter I described changes IBM made to the Express version of the Lotus Notes product. By restoring a key capability to the Express package, we believed we could increase sales and satisfaction with Express. After announcing, I learned IBM had not gone far enough.

About four months after the initial announcement, we made more changes, and aligned the product more closely with the enterprise version.

This time, the blog feedback was all positive, with 25 comments filled with superlatives like "excellent," "great job," and "more of the same please!"

We had left just enough of a differentiation between the Express and enterprise product versions to keep the markets mostly intact. In a few cases, we found situations where customers had elected the wrong license type in the first place and addressed those appropriately.

The reason for changing the Express packaging was to make it useful for yet more customers, to grow the business. As an unintended consequence, though, it inadvertently became more appealing for existing clients, all because I was caught up in the emotion of market reaction to my initial announcement.

The story has a happy ending, though; in the first year after we made these changes, Express was selling better than ever.

The sport of product management is every bit as sophisticated as the coach's job in any team activity. Calling the right plays for offense or defense, at the right time, with the correct strength and volume, and predicting the outcome are the key steps to winning. After all, every product manager wants to make the game-winning play!

Lessons Learned

- Social product managers must conduct a situation analysis and plan their engagement in social networks.

- Social product managers must determine the best possible timing for their message to the market.

- The social product manager must consider the inbound and outbound volume of input and commentary on a given topic and determine a commensurate proactive or reactive response.

- The social product manager must see the big picture and anticipate potential consequences, including unintended ones, prior to engaging.

Endnotes

1 Tom Duff, on EdBrill.com, "Roadmap for Notes/Domino From Here,"
   October 6, 2011 (www.edbrill.com/ebrill/edbrill.nsf/dx/
   roadmap-for-notesdomino-from-here). Used with permission.
2 Paul Mooney, pmooney.net, "IBM — Sort out your software
   downloads!" March 3, 2009 (http://tinyurl.com/9ya9hta). Used with
   permission.
3 Blog post on EdBrill.com, "I am fixing some IBM downloads
   challenges, starting with filenames"
   (www.edbrill.com/ebrill/edbrill.nsf/dx/i-am-fixing-some-ibm-
   downloads-challenges-starting-with-filenames).
4 Blog post on EdBrill.com, "A holiday present — Clustering in
   Domino Collaboration Express." (www.edbrill.com/ebrill/
   edbrill.nsf/dx/
   a-holiday-present-clustering-in-domino-collaboration-express).
5 David Carr, *Information Week,* "Jive CEO: Social Tools Are Essential,
   Not Extras," February 3, 2012 (http://tinyurl.com/
   6som7e7).
6 Mikkel Flindt Heisterberg, "The Distance between IBM and me,"
   January 31, 2006 (www.edbrill.com/ebrill/edbrill.nsf/dx/the-
   distance-between-ibm-and-me). Used with permission.

5

Picking a Fight

It is stated plainly in the IBM Social Computing Guidelines (Appendix A), "Don't pick fights."

So why a whole chapter on something that the Guidelines—which I helped write—explicitly say *not* to do?

The Guidelines themselves provide the answer: Sometimes, it is necessary to address misrepresentations factually. Sometimes, the market needs assurance that even dissenting voices are heard. Sometimes, it is even appropriate to engage directly in debate.

This chapter is about the delicate balance a social business faces between dialogue and diatribe. "Picking a Fight" delves deeper into the wildcards of social networking—"flame wars," trolls, and baiting. (I define these terms along the way.) Conversely, the chapter also examines the decision to say or do nothing, or when actions speak louder than words.

Picking a fight is absolutely permissible in the context of social business, when it can be done factually and professionally. However, the four principles from Chapter 4, "Offense or Defense," need to be carefully applied. What is the situation? What timing will be effective? How loud of a call to action is needed? What are the unintended consequences?

In this chapter, I discuss the art of online debate from two originators—first, from the point of view of the social product manager; and then second, from the perspective of the customer/partner/competitor. Regardless of who starts a fight, key principles apply to the social product manager and, of course, lessons learned.

You Can't Please All of the People...

Humans love to debate. One of the great empowerment aspects of social business tools is the ability for more voices to express opinion, bias, or perspective. There are often just as many exclamations in response, usually in short order. Nobody likes to show up at an Internet fight a week after it happened. The debate is instantaneous, potentially rancorous, then over. Themes and flashpoints may reappear, but the duration of any particular battle is usually short and intense.

Yet words last forever, so it is important to choose the right words and the right overall message when starting a fight.

What are some circumstances where the social product manager might start a fight? Here are some opportunities:

- **Take a contrary position to news of the day.** When a competitor makes a product announcement, often the initial news coverage contains only the vendor's point of view, and perhaps their chosen analysts and customers to endorse that point of view. Most journalists begin to seek the balanced story only as a follow-up to initial news coverage. Instead of waiting for analysis by a third-party influencer or analyst, the social product manager can immediately seize the opportunity to begin a counterspin, ensuring that the market at large recognizes that there is more than one side of the story.

- **Preempt news or announcements.** This is a time-honored marketplace tactic, anticipating an event or milestone. Often, the social product manager uses a preemptive engagement from a defensive stance, as a way to diminish the impact of an impending situation.

- **Discovery of information which will help inform the market.** Used more in politics than in business, this method of uncovering buried and potentially damaging information contributes to the overall body of knowledge around a product category or competitor's product.

■ **Attack an inaccuracy articulated by the media, a competitor, an analyst, or other third party.** Even though traditional marketing and communications principles often suggest avoiding these skirmishes, social product managers can engage in a more tactical battle on a narrower field. The tools of social business, used properly, can be applied as a more surgical approach to debate or diffusion.

You probably noticed that many of these reasons for starting a fight pertain to competition. In that context, my advice to start a fight may seem surprising; IBM as a company prides itself in taking the "high road," limiting attacks on adversaries.

Social media has opened up a narrow vector where culturally we now consider picking a fight acceptable. Our guidelines say:

> *When you see misrepresentations made about IBM by media, analysts or by other bloggers, you may certainly use your blog—or add comments on the original discussion—to point that out. Always do so with respect, stick to the facts and identify your appropriate affiliation to IBM. Also, if you speak about a competitor, you must make sure that what you say is factual and that it does not disparage the competitor.*

Now, as individual voices, an employee engaging in debate does not necessarily carry the full weight of the company into battle. In some ways, product and brand managers must now be prepared to aggressively defend or carefully attack when a clear need exists. The high road is fine to stay above the fray, but sometimes a credible engagement is the only way to move the market forward.

Here are two examples of fights I've started, and then I discuss the reasons for engaging in these ways online.

A Battle with Microsoft

In the old days of competitive intelligence gathering, the only real way for technology competitors to assess their adversaries was to install their products themselves and attend their adversaries' conferences to hear what they told customers. Therefore, in 2004, I found myself in the audience at a Microsoft event, listening to one of their senior executives deliver a session intended to outline the future of his product. The presentation was light on specifics.

Toward the end of his presentation, the Microsoft official turned the tables and offered several minutes of criticism about IBM and Lotus Notes. He claimed the future of Notes was uncertain, and suggested that IBM customers should consider Microsoft for various reasons.

It was time to pick a fight. On my blog, on May 25, 2004, I published a summary of the presentation I had just heard and challenged Microsoft's professionalism:

> *How dare Microsoft criticize... IBM... when they offer their {customers only} a bunch of general future feature goals.*

In 2004, we didn't have the Social Computing Guidelines, and what I wrote was perhaps overly aggressive. However, it had the intended effect, as IT publication *Network World* noticed the skirmish. Based on the comments on my blog, the reporter contacted IBM and asked me to provide a quote countering Microsoft's criticisms. In the published story, *Network World* ran the quote and then went on to describe the Microsoft product's future as having only a "vague roadmap."[1]

A successful skirmish; instead of telling Microsoft's lopsided story, the press had sought out balance and even given IBM a chance to counterpunch.

A Fight with an IT Industry Analyst Firm

In 2010, a large and well-known IT industry analyst firm was planning to publish a paper offering commentary on whether Notes was losing customers to the competition. The analysis itself was relatively balanced, and by the firm's own admission based only on inquiries from their own clients—rather than on a broad market survey. Unfortunately, someone in their organization decided to assign a provocative title to the report, one that conveyed a sense that the analyst was endorsing the competitive product.

As is common in the IT industry, IBM had received a preview of the report and as such could anticipate the noise our competitors would make, simply by pointing to the analyst's website and the title of the report. It wouldn't matter if IT decision makers actually read the report; the headline alone would become a truism.

I decided to take the unusual step of trying to minimize the report's impact in the market by calling attention to it at the very moment it was published. Of course, the provocative title used by the analyst firm was ignored. Instead, I used my blog and Twitter to highlight one of the conclusions in the report: Customers switching to the competition will likely be disappointed. Skirting right up against the edge of the notion of "fair use" in copyright law,[2] I quoted a few balanced components of the report on my blog. The message to readers was that there was no point in giving in to the provocative headline since the report itself lacked alignment with the title.

The analyst firm, perhaps feeling that they would attract less attention in the absence of controversy, tried quickly to counterattack. Their online discussion tried to slant the report toward the headline and criticize me personally rather than defend their report. IBM colleagues and management were prepared for the possibility that we would be criticized for our approach, but we had stuck to the facts.

On the analyst's website, comments on their blog posting criticized them for bias, while my original attack was met only with encouragement. It seemed that the market was tired of induced controversy in this segment.

For this debate, I also used internal social tools. A posted alert to the sales community on our IBM Connections environment gave them the opportunity to prepare for potential customer inquiries and to outreach proactively to those clients who typically relied on the analyst for counsel.

The uproar was over quickly. This analyst's report never surfaced in customer discussions, unlike others where IBM is often asked for our "response." By precisely and immediately timing a preemptive strike, we dissipated a situation before it ever developed.

Picking Fights in Hindsight

Starting both these fights served a valuable purpose. In the case of the first, which was more offensive in nature, my strategy was to offer a longer-term perspective on the competition's announcements, laced with some details they often left out. The objective, which was accomplished once the IT trade press picked up the story, was to diminish the effectiveness of their announcement and raise concerns in potential buyer's minds.

In the second, which was clearly more defensive, my strategy was to likewise reveal that there was more to the story than the headlines conveyed. My goal was to either restore balance to a one-sided communication or, even better, diminish its impact. This situation happened to play out better than anticipated, but picking the fight would have been just as useful had it only served to minimize amplification of the report.

In both cases, the concept of "fear, uncertainty, and doubt" came into play. In IT, decisions about technology adoption are as much about managing risk as they are about the product capabilities themselves. IT buyers often worry about whether a chosen product will stand the test of time, be easily supported, and have a vendor's strength behind it. Any concern about a product's future will raise questions of risk in the IT manager's mind. Much as we like to take the high road, there is a balance between doing so and a sense of conveying fair and correct information in the market. That is why the IBM Social Computing Guidelines say a fight is okay as long as what is said is factually correct. Just don't let it turn into a brawl.

Entering a Fray

It has become a mainstay of the Internet (see Figure 5.1).

Figure 5.1   xkcd.com #386, by Randall Monroe.

Engaging your critics is one of the more challenging skills required in a successful social business. Marketers prefer to control the message and the tone of external communication about your product and organization. When you leave the confines of your company's owned media, such as your website and external presence, or participate in internal discussions, communities, or feedback channels, the social product manager can find themselves in uncharted territory, without support from marketing or the proper defenses against hostility.

Should you engage at all? My answer is yes, with some qualifiers. First, only when the conversation is professional; second, when it is mainstream; and third, only with a defined exit strategy.

Why join in a conflict? Because it will show that you are *engaged* in the market. It might not always lead to a better outcome, but it will build goodwill for those who are participants and, more importantly, observers of the interaction.

There is a bit of politics involved in joining a battle. Sometimes, your intended audience isn't really the person or people criticizing you, but rather those around them. You can view this form of picking a fight as really being about delivering and staying on message. Often, the silent majority—those reading and not interacting—is the real audience for the social product manager and may be the group that is important to win over through engagement. The critic might be at best neutralized, but the silent majority may be positively impacted by your participation.

Sometimes, it is even acceptable to make enemies in the process. No product or brand has ever earned 100 percent customer satisfaction. In internal social interactions, being provocative in a community or forum serves the same purpose as the "devil's advocate" role in a meeting—to get people outside their comfort zone and provide critical thinking.

A professional debate is one where participants focus on topic rather than personality, use respectful language, and further collective understanding through discussion. It is not taking inflammatory bait from Internet trolls or hiding behind anonymous screen names (more on trolls and flames later).

On my blog, I established and published a policy early on that comments needed to be provided with the poster's real name and a valid email address. The email address would not be visible, but could be used to validate that the comment was attached to a professional. Unsurprisingly, the most heavily critical comments over the years have come with names like Fred Flintstone and email addresses like nobody@nobody.com. I quickly delete those.

The real name policy may inhibit some who would like to contribute but are afraid that their comment will live on in Google searches. By the same token, it thus forces those providing feedback to be prepared to stand behind their words, leading to much higher-quality interaction overall.

The fight is not always worth joining. The outcome can be dissatisfying. In May 2009, a blog entry on bynkii.com drew me into a fight. Bynkii is the personal blog of an IT administrator. His real name, John Welch, is attached to the site, but he makes no representation of it as anything other than his own opinion. It is a trash-talking, foul-mouthed blog, but somehow he has built a unique audience within a particular technology market segment.

Welch attracted my attention through a blog entry criticizing Lotus Notes. Several of his readers contacted me about the posting, telling me how influential the website was in certain IT circles. I felt compelled to try to address his criticisms, which were based on an older version of Notes installed in a configuration that was relatively unusual.

The response was personal and vitriolic. Never before had I recoiled from the way an online interaction unfolded. Welch would not be challenged on his home turf. Unfortunately, I had entered battle without an exit strategy, and was now simply forced to retreat.

By then, others had joined the conversation, and each one was being attacked in turn. Nothing was going to be gained, and in fact Welch eventually launched yet further criticisms.

In response to the interaction with Welch, co-founder of OpenNTF.org and IBM Champion Nathan T. Freeman wrote a blog post, which I then linked to from edbrill.com:

> *There are two reasons to offer criticism on any subject in public: 1) to affect a change in behavior or outcome on the part of whoever you're criticizing. 2) to display your criticism for an audience for whom the criticism is an end in itself.*
>
> *The difference between these two objectives is almost always tone. A civil tone signals to the subject of criticism that you have the first purpose. A profane tone signals to the subject that you have the second purpose....So if someone offers public criticism that's filled with vulgarity and vitriol, is there any reason to engage them? They might as well be waving a flag that "I am doing this so people will think I'm cool. I don't really want to change anything."[3]*

The Bynkii discussion was, at the time, visible enough within a specialized community that it seemed worth joining the fight. Among the lessons learned, though, was the idea that a debate may be worth engaging in only if there is truly the opportunity for discussion in a relevant market segment or the mainstream where your buyers and influencers live. It is also critical to define the time to extract from a fight, though perhaps not to disengage entirely. Determine the methods possible to remain a spectator while backing away quietly, just as you might in a real-life conflict.

When a product has tens of millions of end users, it is bound to have some dissenters. With blogs, Twitter, and LinkedIn, some of those individual voices have a way to reach larger audiences. They might also be fringe opinions in a large market, but a more mainstream channel might bring the fringe to the center. At times, this might add weight to a situation analysis where the social product manager chooses to engage at the edge of relevancy, in an attempt to quell a small situation before it enlarges.

Community managers are often taught to look for relevant keywords or product mentions in these venues. Often, it has been suggested that IBM should be looking out for mentions of our commercial products on Twitter and engaging with those tweets.

There are clear benefits to doing so, because many happy users do express their joy and appreciation for our products. Giving those supporters amplification is the topic of Chapter 6, "Activate Your Advocates."

Connecting with critics, though, isn't always worthwhile. Frustrated end users might or might not be persons of influence, but their scope of influence may be limited beyond their own organization. Engaging every critic has the unintended consequence of encouraging more critics, who know that they have obtained the vendor's attention.

However, when the criticism is a mainstream voice—a reporter, a prominent blogger, or public figure—it is often worth engaging. It's especially important in this scenario to consider the right approach, your company's social networking guidelines, and even your public relations staff and their relationships. Still, opting in to the discussion can often pay off.

In 2008, hearings in the United States Congress were investigating the disappearance of public records. In the transition to a new email system in one government branch, several million emails—part of the historical recording of government—had been lost. Those emails had been sent via Lotus Notes.

During the hearing, Congressman Darrell Issa of California made statements to the effect of blaming the email system, rather than any procedural error. His comments were reported in the public record. They were not very flattering.

The situation analysis was clear: It would be damaging to have an elected official on record as blaming the product. The timing was critical because the statements could quickly spread. The volume had the potential to explode, as the mainstream press was reporting on the hearings.

Instead of starting with social media in response, I went the traditional route. This was clearly a sensitive situation, and no obscure blog post was going to be the right answer. Instead, I contacted IBM's government relations organization, who contacted the congressman's office.

Within hours, I was on the phone with Congressman Issa himself. Issa needed less than five minutes to understand that the issues being discussed before Congress were implementation related. He apologized and agreed to make the situation right.

Congressman Issa had the public record corrected, issued IBM a letter of clarification, and continued the excellent relationship he had with IBM overall. In subsequent hearings, he demonstrated understanding of the technology to a far deeper level.

At that point, I was able to turn social. A blog entry described the interactions and the resolution, in the context of the current event. No further discussion about the role of the particular software product occurred; from there, the public discourse was only about the implementation. What could have been a very damaging *non sequitur* simply evaporated.

A few lessons were learned from this event. The first was the need to detect potential flare-ups in the market. Listening to customers and the ecosystem talk among themselves often reveals issues that are building into potentially larger problems. The second was the need to choose the right supporting team when picking a fight, as a result of the situation analysis. Clearly, the criticism of Lotus Notes could have just been ignored. However, because it had attracted attention, it was important not to let it stand. With the right team, and the right situation analysis, the right approach was launched—and the situation resolved, quickly.

Sometimes, the fight is more about principles. Again, recognizing that entering a discussion comes with risks, where it makes sense to set the record straight and the audience is one where that will matter, factual corrections can be critical and important.

In July 2009, a start-up consulting firm authored ten reasons for organizations using Lotus Notes to consider Google's new Google Apps. Most were written tongue-in-cheek, using an agitating style to attract readers to the punch line, a seminar invitation on the same topic.

It would have been easy to ignore the new firm, but their coordinated marketing campaign was attracting attention. IBM customers were asking for a response. In commenting on the ten reasons, I used the opportunity to position IBM's new cloud service—a direct competitor to Google Apps. It was also a chance to reframe the discussion in broader terms than just replacing one email system with another, describing that IBM's solutions offered a complete platform for social business. I also then linked to the discussion from my own blog and Twitter.

Taking the steam out of the attack worked. Only two prospective customers attended the firm's seminar. One of the speakers backed out. Three years later, Google has less than 1 percent of the enterprise email market, according to IDC, as their initially strong entry to the market was diffused by factual dissection.

Make Some Enemies

The last component of this chapter is a little unorthodox and uncomfortable but is important to cover. To move ahead, an engaged and transparent social product manager sometimes needs to make some people unhappy.

This is one step further than starting or entering a fight. Here I am talking about isolating the fighter.

Most of the time, the adage goes, it's not worth wrestling with a pig. You both get dirty, while the pig enjoys it. The saying often appears in online discussion referring to that unique type of Internet character: the troll.

Trolls are your worst critics, those who are deliberately inflammatory and vitriolic, repeatedly surfacing their criticisms regardless of their relevance or merit. Their barbs are likely to feel personal to the product manager, who often has the responsibility for the decisions that created whatever complaint the trolls had in the first place.

Some trolls are persistent in nature. They exist to stir up trouble, perhaps not just for your product, but for your entire industry. Trolls may even strive for a sort of digital reputation of their own, attempting to set up a good versus evil battle.

In most cases, trolls are best ignored. Even the Wikipedia entry on trolls is titled "Do not feed the troll." Sometimes, though, there is value to isolating them.

When a troll's comments are clearly outside the mainstream, it may prove valuable, once, to identify them as such. The importance of this is not to validate—or feed—the troll, but rather to marginalize the troll's influence on the community and conversation.

In other words, by validating trolls just one time, you can actually invalidate them, if done in the right manner.

Usually the way to do this is offline. Entering the fray with a troll is pig wrestling. Instead, find a way to connect with your troll—email is usually the least-emotional approach, though Twitter or even a phone call might be more effective—and present the troll with an action. It might be positive or punitive, depending on the desired outcome. A positive contact may elicit their sought-after validation, although it can encourage future trolling. A punitive contact may cause some damage with fallout but likely will be the end of the trolling.

It is really important to emphasize avoiding a public fight with trolls. Whenever I have failed to do so, I have ended up dirty from the pig wrestling. I have learned the lesson to handle these discussions privately, if at all.

A risk exists that trolls might take engagement as a sign of validation. They might even choose to publish the private communication. It is important never to attack trolls on an individual or personal level, instead sticking to the facts unemotionally.

What trolling has risen to the level where it cannot be ignored? The primary examples I have are when the trolling gets personal and the troll is known to have some level of influence on other customers, partners, or community members. Here are three:

- When I have been criticized for not affecting desired change at IBM—whether or not that change makes sense for IBM
- When my development team has been called names (or even expletives) for gaps in their product functionality
- When the trolls take it upon themselves to try to represent me or my company and do so incorrectly

Most of this book features specific examples or case studies. For this topic, however, it seems to make little sense to tell such a story. Simply, in cases like these, the troll is contacted and usually warned about current/future consequences. Such contact usually ends the trolling. At a minimum, it has usually lowered their volume and amplification. It also sets a bit of an example for the spectators of the fight. Transgressions that prompt consequences for the troll usually occur on a social network or in an otherwise visible manner. When contact affects a change in behavior, others who have witnessed the trolling may realize that it could have negative consequences.

In no way should this be taken as advocacy for spending a lot of time on trolls. I've not enjoyed any of the troll fighting over the past decade. It has really only risen to this level of intervention a few times. Most days, I love being able to talk directly to my customers, partners, and even competitors. I jump in again every morning, focused on new opportunities and excitement.

This chapter and the preceding one have focused on some of the negative and defensive situations that occur in a social business. From here, *Opting In* transitions to pure offense: how to activate the tools of social business to your strongest potential.

However, this detour into defense and online conflict has been critically important. Social business has opened up the conversation with your customers, partners, suppliers, reporters, analysts, and competitors. As a product or brand manager, you have a choice whether to opt in to that conversation—but either way, the conversation is going to continue.

There are times to let a conflict go. During the writing of this book, an IT industry analyst whom I respect is using Twitter to often criticize a U.S.-based airline. His hope seems to be that the right people at the airline will read his comments and do something to improve customer service. Most of these grievances, in my opinion, are already known, though, so the marginal impact may be low. It certainly is highly unlikely the airline will suddenly one day use its Twitter account to tell the analyst, "Gee, you are right; we are screwing up!" Those kind of candid admissions cost people jobs, drive stock prices lower, and deflate consumer confidence. The airline realizes it is better for even a somewhat-amplified stream of complaints to file into its organization than it is to enter the fray.

My hope, though, is that the airline's product managers are using the influx of negative feedback as catalysts for change inside their organization. Constructive criticism, via the voice of the customer, can often be stronger than internal demonstrable expertise.

Jacob Share, founder and senior vice president of Share Select Media, encourages readers to listen to criticism. In an entry on the Personal Branding blog, he says the following:

Once you can discern when the message is one you really should listen to, you'll grow much quicker.[4]

Lessons Learned

- Social product managers now have more flexibility with regard to the message and medium than with traditional marketing and communications tools and can start fights effectively.

- Entering the fray of an existing fight is more perilous, and is something social product managers should often avoid doing. However, the right situation analysis and plan can result in beneficial outcomes such as ending the fight, neutralizing the fighter, or influencing the silent majority.

- Although in the world of social media people are more apt to criticize than to congratulate, social product managers can influence product/service perception through professional engagement in mainstream debate.

Endnotes

[1] *Network World,* "Microsoft detours Exchange direction," May 31, 2004 (www.networkworld.com/news/2004/0531teched.html?page=2).

[2] *Fair use* is a doctrine in U.S. copyright law that reproduction of a copyrighted work may be acceptable without permission of the copyright holder. (www.copyright.gov/fls/fl102.html).

[3] Nathan T. Freeman, "On Tone and Civility" February 19, 2009 (http://tinyurl.com/8d6csnr). Used with permission.

[4] Jacob Share (twitter: @jacobshare), "Constructive Criticism or Compliments: Which Builds Your Brand Better?" June 10, 2011 (http://tinyurl.com/92th2z8). Used with permission.

6

Activate Your Advocates

Product management is an influence discipline.

Because product and brand managers typically have little direct-line authority over budget or resource, catalyzing others to act in a desired way is the name of the game. This is true both inside your organization and, for the social product manager, externally as well.

The product manager is typically the de facto leader of a federated organization, with each individual participant acting on independent thinking but sharing common ideas and objectives. This chapter explores how to activate your advocates as influencers. Both internal and external people you touch are also influencers—on colleagues, customers, prospects, and industry figures.

To emphasize the point, many of the insights in this chapter and beyond originate from influencers: IBM customers, partners who make their living through IBM technology, or IBMers who are not product managers. All of these contributors volunteered to write about the social product manager from their own point of view. As a bonus, their participation originated socially, after learning about this book project online.

Leadership

Product management leadership is about more than your title. In any organization and market, a product manager has to develop credibility and authority through good ideas, excellent communication, and solid data or supporting evidence. Building a following—those internally and externally tuned into the product manager's thoughts and ideas—takes time. Success comes through building a track record of reliable, beneficial ideas and decisions, and ultimately delivers positive results for your product and the individuals who help build it and deliver it Your network and organization are more likely to be influenced and follow your leadership when you take them on a path of proven success.

Social business leadership is more than simply getting on Twitter, starting a Facebook page, and creating a blog. The core social business principle of *engagement* reenters the equation. Engagement that results in interactive dialogue, both externally and internally, is a key foundation for success. All too often, ineffective marketers and product managers use these social tools as check box activities, believing that if they tweet a link or post a blog entry they are being "social." Instead, two-way communication is the basis for building a following.

The *unique voice* of the social product manager offers the opportunity to build credibility and, therefore, audience. Your communication through social networks, internally and externally, needs to offer differentiated value for others to choose to pay attention. If you are sharing files (inside or outside) your organization, they should offer more than just standard marketing messages.

The more you provide information and insight that nobody else provides, the more influence and audience you will build. A successful leader can then convert that audience into extensions of the social product manager—having an army of advocates who will engage in offense or defense, pick a fight, or simply amplify messages to even broader markets and audiences.

Content Versus Curation

Valuable content will find an audience. Google and other search engines guarantee it. Society today has come to completely rely on these magic websites, which locate relevant information on any topic in mere milliseconds.

Search engine optimization, a marketing tool for several years, is no longer the magic potion enabling corporate websites to insert their content into the buyer's decision-making process. Increasingly, search results will guide a buyer somewhere other than a company's self-provided marketing material; more likely, the destination will be informed content from humans.

For example, as a society, we used to rely mostly on travel agents or published brochures to tell us which hotels to use when traveling. Today, a simple search query leads to potential accommodation.

Searching for a hotel might land on Hilton.com, but it could also land on booking.com, TripAdvisor, Yelp, or countless other sites that provide vehicles for customer feedback. The hotel can no longer rely on glossy photos or cozy relationships to bring them business; they simply must provide a good product and compel their customers to be vocal about it.

At IBM, we recognize the need for humans to curate all the information available from our organization. In the past, marketing's primary objective was to bring potential clients to the pages of IBM.com. Today, there is recognition that every buyer begins his or her journey through search, typically focused on earned media, rather than vendor insertion into their path through paid media such as advertising.

One of the benefits of encouraging all IBMers to participate in social networks is that those unique voices provide individual perspective and valuable insight into our offerings and solutions. Product managers, developers, sales engineers, and consultants can all add their own perspective to IBM product news, documentation, and resources.

As an example, during a 19-day period in June 2012, IBM's own Unica® enterprise marketing management tool[1] was used to monitor referral clicks from EdBrill.com that landed somewhere on IBM.com. During this time, nearly half of all tracked registrations for a set of particular IBM.com "events"—such as downloads, white papers, or other marketing collateral— were completed by readers who started their visit to IBM.com coming in from EdBrill.com. More than 900 such event engagements took place over the 19 days. Another 149 event engagements occurred as a result of inbound referral from other influencer blogs, with content similar to EdBrill.com.

The results were interesting, and surprising to me. Something about the content on my blog was attracting engaged readers. About half of all EdBrill.com visits originate from Google searches, meaning they are not regular readers of the site. The information provided on EdBrill.com was sufficiently appealing that they then clicked through to a linked page on IBM.com containing additional information. The IBM.com page subsequently offered something that was valuable enough for the reader to take an action.

The credibility and authority of EdBrill.com created the opportunity for positive results on IBM.com. Although it happens to be my own blog, it falls into the category of earned, rather than owned, media. I am personally as in control of what I write about as any other blogger. The blog content is a deliberate choice of using authentic voice when it is the right time and topic, not simply echoing party lines.

The lesson learned: *Humans want to learn from other humans.* Prospects, buyers, and advocates listen to and take guidance from trusted sources. Therefore, it is critical to empower proponents with the right information, tools, and credibility to share their insight in ways that result in meaningful interactions.

Any product or service has someone in the marketplace who enjoys advocating for it. Usually these supporters are directly connected to the product—customers, suppliers, vendors, or partners. Among a potentially infinite number of people, especially for consumer products, finding those that love your product enough to tell the world about it is a challenging task.

Today, many tools in the market do sentiment analysis of online social networks. IBM's Cognos® Consumer Insight (www-01.ibm.com/software/analytics/cognos/analytic-applications/consumer-insight/) can pinpoint key influencers as part of both traditional and digital marketing activities. These tools are especially useful in broad horizontal or consumer markets.

Analytics, customer relationship management (CRM) systems, and voice of the customer (VOC) tools can be used to understand your advocates and measure their level of influence. These systems all feed into marketing efforts, where you can develop care and feeding systems such as newsletters, Twitter IDs, Facebook fan pages, event invitations, and other standard marketing tools.

For the social product manager, though, harvesting the cream of the crop among all your advocates becomes a very personal exercise. Sometimes, you will want your outbound communication to use all those marketing vehicles, such as broad announcements and new product introductions. Then there are other opportunities best kept to a chosen few. The brand manager needs to clearly identify and classify their most important influencers, a ready "go to" list of top voices. Selecting those supporters is up to you.

Identifying Influencers and Providing Recognition

Previous chapters have discussed the importance of personal branding. Your advocates might not think of themselves in this way, though. Creating programs and activities which reward those advocates is a key to activating them. The more you can engage those who are most effective at telling your story, the more symbiotic the relationships become.

Of course, there is both benefit and investment needed on both sides.

Our experience at IBM shows that providing access to insider information or to our engineering staff motivates advocates to take action. For example, for many years, my team and I conducted traditional product design reviews. These were face-to-face mini-conferences, with 50 to 100 invited participants. We drew the audience from those who were most active at providing feedback on our products, creating a circular relationship where we gave more information to those who were giving more to us.

This method of selection was useful, but imperfect. It tended to reward the person speaking the loudest or most often, rather than the most insightful. Over time, the need to add a little process to the equation was recognized.

Today, instead of conducting design reviews, a formal design partner program exists. Participation in the program is by nomination only. Nominations can come from product management, development, or sales functions, not from the customer or partner/vendor themselves. Because the companies and individuals who are part of the program had to be formally evaluated before being included, there is an increased level of expectation on both sides.

The result is extremely positive. By providing the opportunity for early bidirectional feedback on new products, better software comes out of our labs. A ready-made force of product advocates is created, too, as the design partners themselves feel a sense of ownership when features they asked for are released into the market. Design partners also increase the visibility of the IBM solution and themselves, within their own organization, building their own reputation, influence, and leadership.

Carrying the title IBM Design Partner was useful to build credibility for some of our advocates, but not every supporter could afford the time commitment to work with early stage, prerelease software required by the program. Therefore, other programs and venues have become part of the product design and advocacy process. Enter the IBM Champions, a program created in 2011 to publicly identify and endorse IBM's strongest advocates.

JOYCE DAVIS ON THE IBM CHAMPION PROGRAM

Joyce Davis is a community manager at IBM, and one of the leaders of the IBM Champion program.

Community input is critical to ensure that the products IBM creates meet the needs of our clients and partners. Equally important is the engagement of evangelists, advocates in the community to help demonstrate the value of our solutions in the marketplace and to drive product adoption.

The IBM Champion program (ibm.com/champion) identifies key external experts and thought leaders who are community leaders: generous forum contributors, conference speakers, technical authors, user group leaders, bloggers, and podcasters. They share their product knowledge and expertise, encouraging the use of IBM solutions, and reaching out to help the community of customers utilizing those solutions. Much of this advocacy work is done on their own time, outside regular job responsibilities, and often at their own personal expense.

Community recognition programs are by no means new or unique to IBM. However, as a company we understood the importance of recognizing outstanding community members. We wanted to raise their visibility and help foster their passion to do what they do best—advocate for IBM solutions and grow the community. Since recommendations from trusted sources are a key factor in the IT decision making process, we wanted to ensure that these credible experts had the visibility they need to make a difference.

The IBM Champion program was introduced as a formal way to recognize those who go above and beyond to evangelize IBM products, share their technical expertise, and expand the community of professionals focused on IBM solutions. The elite group of Champions (none of whom work for IBM) is chosen by an IBM committee based on nominations from the community. In return for their valuable contributions, our Champions receive increased visibility on IBM websites, invitations and discounts to IBM events, previews under nondisclosure agreements, public recognition at conferences, access to key IBM business executives and technical leaders, and IBM Champion-branded merchandise. (Do not underestimate the impact of a high quality jacket!) They also obtain the use of the official IBM Champion digital badge—a graphic they can add to their email signature, post on their website, or print on business cards. IBM Champions serve a one-year term and are re-evaluated annually.

The program also serves as motivation for aspiring champions to increase their community efforts in hopes that they can be recognized as an IBM Champion in the future.

Because of their increased exposure, IBM Champions are sought after by companies worldwide to share their expertise and provide an objective viewpoint on IBM solutions. Many are invited to meetings where various solutions are being evaluated. The program also drives increased participation and input from the broader community.

> *"The IBM Champion program has increased my visibility and standing within the community. It has connected me with a broader set of experts both inside and outside of IBM and it's enabled me to become more effective at solving real business issues (on a worldwide basis!)."*
>
> *—Simon Vaughan, IBM Champion, Cardiff University. Used by permission.*

In addition to recognition, the program offers an ongoing path of communication between the Champions and IBM leaders, fostering trust and encouraging honest communication. As a result, product teams are more willing to share information such as product direction with these experts. In turn, the Champions provide invaluable insight into what our customers want and need. They serve as a pulse on the community and steer IBM toward the best and most effective strategies to reach a broad set of customers with the right solutions. This increased participation in the product development process is a key way in which IBM teams with our partners and customers to demonstrate the value of social business.

The IBM Champion program is one way IBM cultivates a spirit of collaboration and community, essential elements of social business.

Although the IBM Champion program is designed and run by marketing, the social product manager reaps the benefits. The Champions are a ready-made audience for early briefings, insight, and feedback.

In 2011, when we decided to bundle together some of our software capabilities and provide them at no additional charge to a set of existing customers, the Champions were the first audience to hear about it. Under nondisclosure, the Champions were briefed on the upcoming product announcement.

The hour-long e-meeting allowed attendees to see each other online, as well as participate in an open group chat as the e-meeting unfolded. The social nature of the interaction, among Champions, as well as between Champions and IBMers, created much more value than an outbound-only briefing.

This seems like a standard product management tactic to conduct early disclosure, but there are some very specific reasons for highlighting the briefing here.

First, the special invite-only event created a sense of intimacy beyond the usual briefing. Attendees recognized they were seeing a first glimpse of something that would eventually be more broadly shared and treated the information accordingly.

Second, the IBM product management team received early feedback on their proposed messages and were able to refine them before public announcement. While the Champions are all supporters, they also offered candid input as to where the story could be improved. Because this was done in a group setting, they were able to iterate off each other's ideas and input, resulting in specific and actionable direction back to IBM.

Third, the Champions were now primed to tell IBM's story, both to the market at large as well as inside their organizations, upon public announcement. In some cases, we even knew or had influenced what to expect they would say because they had already shared their reactions in advance. Preparations to highlight Champion reactions on the day of announcement, to amplify the message, could be put in place proactively by IBM's Marketing team.

In no place do we set an expectation that the Champions will in fact be publicly vocal upon announcement of news. Internal influence alone may be a valuable result. By providing an intimate, bidirectional, advance interaction, a more-desirable outcome is that our key advocates will participate in the dissemination of news and opinion. Often, they deliver. They adopt the most important attribute in telling the story, too: unique voice.

If all we did was get an army of people to retweet an announcement, it would be helpful but not particularly useful or even genuine. That the Champions can tell the story from their own point of view creates engagement in the marketplace, not just repetition.

Continuous Feedback

The philosophy of activating advocates has to be a continuous, conscious effort, not just when launching a product. Too often the tools of social networking appear to be "check box" activities around the time of new product introduction. While, as described previously, release-related activity can drive engagement, everyday activities can as well.

For example, the product designers for IBM Lotus Notes version 8 faced a challenge. Their mission was to completely modernize the product's user interface, or UI. Nearly the entire focus of the new release was the updated UI, so the design team was front and center of the activity during product development. Design is a very subjective aspect of software engineering, and they faced challenges on how to make decisions on the best approach for various UI elements. While taking input from various constituent groups, they also had to ensure that the result was cohesive, greater than the sum of the individual design decisions.

At the time the project started, in 2005, IBM's research and development organization used traditional methods of evaluating the usability of our products. Often, the primary tool was subject observation of an end user working his or her way through proposed approaches to product design. A usability lab was a room with a one-way mirror, with researchers watching as a series of tasks were attempted on the proposed UI.

The lead designer on Lotus Notes 8, Dr. Mary Beth Raven, recognized the opportunity that social networking provided to change the way UI research was conducted. She started a blog, eventually enhanced with other social networking tools, to share proposed design concepts and to actively engage users in the redesign.

This was an unheard of approach in the software industry. Showing potential designs in public, other than through carefully controlled marketing activity, had never been done and carried risk around what kind of expectations it would set for the final product.

Dr. Raven's blogging created some anxiety in our organization. Product developers were not used to having their ideas openly discussed, dissected, and critiqued. Management was concerned whether customers would perceive our experimentation as indecisiveness. Questions arose as to whether the input we would receive from the market would be truly representative. Concern was expressed that we would be "tipping our hand" to competition prematurely.

Undeterred, Dr. Raven and her team eventually published hundreds of blog entries discussing planned or potential new features over the subsequent years. Every one of the blog posts received thousands of visits, as the product's user community itself was engaged in a transparent dialogue around the future of the product. Most important of all, Dr. Raven and her team responded to comments and even posted revisions on designs—revisions made specifically in response to feedback received on the blog.

For example, the design team had planned to have a pop-up dialog asking users if they wanted to automatically add to their workspace any databases that they opened. The response on the blog was an overwhelming: "No, do not ask this bothersome question." So, the design team decided *not* to add the pop-up. Dr. Raven communicated this decision in a blog post long before the product shipped:

"Okay, so, it's pretty clear that this 'ask Samantha if she wants to add a database' is a really unpopular idea. To be fair (to us designers) the mental model we'd been using was that of things like a document—when you go to close it, you get asked if you want to save it. But okay, fine. Browser mental model it is."[2]

A positive benefit was that many, many more customers were "bought in" to the finished product. Every customer who had been part of the discussion of what the product should look like could immediately represent the result to his or her own organization, demonstrating that IBM had listened to the personal feedback and made the product better as a result. This inbound advocacy (directed to IBM) demonstrated the same principal as the outbound advocacy described earlier: Humans listen to humans.

As a result, IBM Lotus Notes 8—actually 8.5.3 at the time of this writing—has proven to command aggressive customer adoption cycles. For Notes 8.5.3, adoption exceeded 70 percent of the customer base within 12 months of delivery, according to IBM tracking studies, download statistics, and technical support calls, far greater than expectations and typical software adoption rates.

Today, many Internet companies do live testing of potential user interface designs, such as the Google "A | B test" method described in Chapter 1, "Why Social Business?" However, the pioneering effort to take the wisdom of the crowds, where potential users could discuss possibilities not just with IBM but with each other, leveraged all three tenets of social business: engaged, transparent, and agile.

GO WHERE YOUR CUSTOMERS ARE

Amy Hoerle is a consultant with Kim Greene Consulting, Inc. She spent the first 13 years of her career at IBM providing support for the Lotus family of products.

How do you reach out to your customers? The answer to that question has certainly changed in the past 10 to 20 years.

Approximately 15 years ago, there was a software bug that IBM wanted to notify customers about and request that they apply a patch. As an IBM employee, I recall asking my manager how the customers would be notified. What was the reply? "Customers will be receiving a letter in the mail." Wow! Can you imagine that happening today?

What about the other direction? How could customers reach IBM? Years ago, if a customer had a message for IBM, he needed to contact support through a toll-free number. As someone who spoke on behalf of IBM at user conferences I would hear, "I really wish IBM would do x." My typical reply was, "That's a great idea! Have you submitted a request for that?" Customers usually responded that the process to call in a request took too much time. Sometimes, I had enough information to move on it anyway, and other times it was, sadly, dropped.

When I first started working in IBM technical support, the documents we produced had a very limited audience. If the answer wasn't in the product documentation, as a customer you had no choice but to call IBM for assistance. A few years down the road, most of the technical documents became available on the Internet for public viewing. However, as great as these documents were, there was no way to see who wrote the article or contact the author for questions.

Now on the outside, over the past few years I have witnessed another shift with IBM technical content. The majority of the information can now be found in wikis, dynamic web pages, published on IBM.com. There are pros and cons with a wiki, but one advantage is that as a customer you can see and potentially interact with the author or even update the information yourself.

Things have changed. IBM's user conferences now offer product requirement request forms in the back of every room. Have something on your mind? Fill out the form and it goes directly to IBM product managers for review. That's a great idea for those who can make it to the conference, but the reality for many is that conferences are no longer part of the annual budget.

These days, you don't have to be in the same place, location, or even time to communicate. This shift is visible when looking at how IBM now communicates with its clients. When looking for information, I used to turn to my favorite search engine, rather than try to look on the IBM website. Now I get new information pushed to me via email, blogs, Facebook, and Twitter. Remember the days when you found out a new product release was available by getting the media in the mail? Not anymore! Now in a few minutes I know a new release is available and see information about the newest tech notes, upcoming community calls, events, and more. I get all of this just by monitoring my Twitter stream.

When I am shopping for a new car, mobile app, or just about anything these days, I want to either "take it for a test drive" or read a review. In IBM's case, it provides a great "try before you buy" resource in the IBM Greenhouse. Prospective customers can take a test drive of IBM Connections, IBM Sametime, or Notes at https://greenhouse.lotus.com.

So, where are your customers and prospects? Are they still backing up in your queues for support, scouring the Internet looking for their answer or are they actively engaged with you? You've now been introduced to several examples of ways that IBM has opened its doors and evolved over the past decade. Now the challenge is yours. How will you revolutionize your business to meet your customers, wherever they may be? Go where your customers are. Be social with them. Engage.

Truth in Use

During the research for this book, I interviewed Ben Edwards, who is IBM's vice president, digital strategy. Edwards described one of the most important tools for activating activists today in selling almost anything: Truth in use.

Consider the fact that buyers no longer solely consider slick collateral and spec sheets to be the tools to evaluate a purchasing decision. Buyers want to be part of an experience, not just fed information. The experience itself matters: how simple, how beautiful, how interactive.

In other words, the buying experience is now in the product or brand manager's realm—the product must speak for itself.

The changing expectation has prompted marketers in both business and consumer markets to adapt quickly. For example, automaker Chevrolet introduced a "love it or return it" policy in the American market in 2012, which grants buyers of a new car a 60-day trial period. The car can be returned within that trial period if the customer is dissatisfied. Money-back guarantees are common with consumer purchases, but never before had a fast-depreciating asset such as an automobile come with no strings attached.

In talking about IBM's opportunities with Edwards, he emphasized the importance of try and buy to the future of software and online services. Edwards mentioned trends such as the consumerization of IT, where end-user expectations of how computers should operate are set based on their access to and experience directly with more software as a consumer. Users then bring that experience to their business environment, demanding easy-to-deploy solutions with low barriers to entry. They also seek the ability to try software out first to evaluate it and then move quickly to a buying decision in as few clicks as possible.

Truth in use demands a change in product management. The product manager needs to be more attuned to word-of-mouth marketing as a desired result of the use of their product. Requirements may be driven not just by the benefit of the product itself but by how naturally it lends itself to advocacy from a buyer, publicly or internally.

Try and buy consumers are natural advocates for the solutions they purchase. They are personally invested in the success of their buying decision and seek to validate those purchases. Upselling or cross-selling opportunities can naturally be presented to these champions, who already have experienced the ease of doing business with your organization.

An important opportunity with satisfied try and buy customers is reference selling. Potential buyers, as every product manager knows, can be influenced by customer references. During my IBM career, I have used the principles of a sales methodology called "solution selling," which focuses on pain points experienced by potential customers and how the product or service on offer can solve those pains.

As a product manager, the typical customer conversation instinctively gravitates toward features and capabilities. Solution selling advocates a discussion in the prospective customer's language instead. One of the best ways to do so is to provide examples of how other customers have addressed their pains through purchase of the product or service. References thus take on a greater value when looked at in the context of a solution sale.

The social product manager has the opportunity to become a more active champion of both reference stories and potential reference customers. Because the main value to potential references is their recognition for making a positive purchase decision, highlighting such references through social media can increase the payback, while also accelerating influence.

During the writing of this chapter, I tweeted a link to an IBM customer case study that had just been published. That tweet was retweeted several times, but I also received a surprising reply, shown in Figure 6.1.

Figure 6.1 Developing a reference.

The partner organization that had submitted the reference story responded only a few hours after the tweet had been published. One simple broadcast had positively reinforced their decision to submit a reference story, and increased their influence as well as mine as a product manager.

In Chapter 7, "Tools of the Trade," I further examine the various channels that the social product manager can utilize to engage with the marketplace.

Lessons Learned

- The social product manager can leverage market advocates to amplify messages and provide unique voice perspectives.

- The social product manager's efforts to recognize and reward advocates will pay returns in carrying market messages further and with additional credibility.

- The social product manager can act as a guide for customers, partners, and other advocates in providing useful content and coordination of unique voices in the marketplace and guiding interaction among those voices.

- The social product manager must adopt to changing market conditions by delivering the right experiences for prospects to move through sales and support processes and turn into satisfied customers.

Endnotes

[1] For more information about IBM's Enterprise Marketing Management solutions, visit www-142.ibm.com/software/products/us/en/category/SWX00.

[2] Dr. Mary Beth Raven, "OK so we WILL NOT be asking users if they want to add databases...," IBM developerWorks user experience design blog, June 27, 2006 (http://tinyurl.com/8rhms78). . Used with permission.

7

Tools of the Trade

Movie director Woody Allen once said that "80 percent of success is just showing up." Social product managers can have a profound impact on their marketplace, their reputation, and their influence, simply through "showing up" and participating.

By opting in to the conversations already taking place about your product, or within your marketplace, you can learn firsthand about trends, interests, pain points, and successes. You can decrease the distance between you and your customers, prospects, suppliers, and partners. You can wield knowledge and data from broad interactions, not just from the last customer meeting in which you participated.

In short, the social product manager can be omnipresent. This chapter explores how, by outlining the tools available and helping to determine when they are appropriate.

The social product manager conducts various tasks online, including listening to the market, discerning credible voices, and building relationships. These are all horizontal activities that you will conduct across the entire marketplace. Yet different tools may be appropriate for each of these different activities. Sometimes more than one tool is needed to accomplish a particular goal or action. Understanding how to choose the right tool or tools, purposefully, is the goal of this chapter.

2011 IBM CMO Study and the Importance of Customer Insight

In 2011, IBM interviewed more than 1,700 chief marketing officers (CMOs) in 19 industries across 64 countries to better understand their goals and the challenges they confront. Although product managers may or may not report into marketing executives, there is a natural alignment around understanding customer requirements and buying patterns.

The IBM CMO study drew several conclusions about the importance of customer insights. The study indicated that the way in which organizations obtain the point of view of the consumer is changing:

> One reason most organizations struggle to get the customer insights they need is that they still focus on understanding markets rather than individuals. At least 80 percent of CMOs rely on traditional sources of information such as market research and competitive benchmarking to make strategic decisions. Similarly, more than 60 percent rely on sales, campaign analysis and the like.
>
> Relatively few CMOs, by contrast, are exploiting the full power of the digital grapevine. Although nearly three-quarters use customer analytics to mine data, only 26 percent are tracking blogs, only 42 percent are tracking third-party reviews and only 48 percent are tracking consumer reviews. This is largely because the tools, processes and metrics they use are not designed to capture and evaluate the unstructured data produced by social platforms.
>
> Yet blogs, consumer reviews and third-party reviews disclose what discrete customers want. They provide a rich source of information about customer sentiment, with context, that can help companies more accurately predict demand patterns.[1]

The high-tech industry, including IBM, offers many analytics solutions designed to help organizations understand the voice of the customer. From sentiment analysis to predictive analytics to targeted campaign messaging tools, CMOs have a plethora of tools at their disposal.

As a practical matter, decisions to implement such solutions tend to be driven by marketing executives, and are acquired for their ability to analyze the entire marketplace, both broad and deep. For this book, my focus is on tactical ways a social product manager can *individually* connect with the market.

Inbound Social Networking Tools

Public social networks form the skeletal system for the social product manager. Each of these sites or services connects people to people in a particular way, usually around a specific focal point: a person, a photograph, a topic. Discussions, feedback, linking, and other interaction grow from that focal point.

Some of the social networks you use in your personal life have applicability in business as well. IBM has a presence on Pintrest, Tumblr, Facebook, Twitter, LinkedIn, Flickr, and many other social networks. This chapter applies a product management lens to each type of network, either from the perspective of inbound (information coming in to the product manager) or outbound (communications originating from the brand manager or organization).

Google Alerts

The basic unit of currency for the social product manager is the Google alert. Google Alerts, found at google.com/alerts, sends you email notifications on a scheduled or real-time basis when there are new Internet items detected by Google's search engine matching your particular criteria.

The Google alert is the secret to ubiquity. Using Google's Boolean logic, you can set up searches for your own name, your product names, your organization or brand names, competitors, marketplace terms, or other relevant content. With those alerts, when there is a news story, new blog, web page, or YouTube video referencing those topics, an email containing a link and summary content will provide awareness and an opportunity to engage (see Figure 7.1).

There are obviously differences in the power and effectiveness of Google Alerts for mass-market versus specialized products. An alert on, for example, "Diet Coke," will be so overwhelming or diluted that the results would be useless. Such an alert could end up referencing any blogger who writes about his enjoyment of a carbonated soda while walking the dog; however, if your product or service is in a more discrete market, using alerts to engage in the conversation is a critical tool.

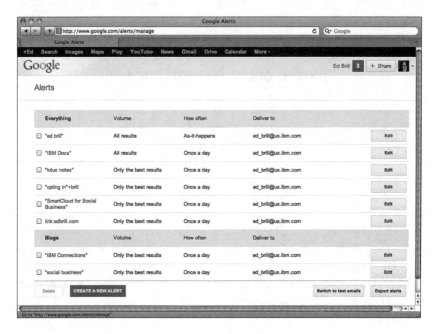

Figure 7.1   Google Alerts.

After deciding to activate Google Alerts, the next decision is what level of engagement to pursue. The lessons on offense versus defense and picking a fight from earlier in the book can be usefully applied. If a blogger writes about your product, do you leave a comment or not? Is timing important? Will it create a different impression on readers if you are first or last to engage?

Determining the appropriate level of engagement is a skill honed over time. Some of the alerts, even with fine-tuned parameters, will turn up low-value content, spam, or other Internet dead ends. These are obviously best ignored. Other alerts will be orthogonal references to your search parameters. Separating the useful from the less useful is a quick task but very worthwhile.

Here are a few tips on using Google Alerts:

- Be sure to put exact quotes around key terms, such as your own name, that are critical to monitor as exact matches.

- Conversely, remember that there are times when the exact match is too narrow of a search. My full given name is on my business card, but I never refer to myself that way. Occasionally, reporters have written news stories quoting "Edward Brill"—which my alerts don't catch.

- You can create an alert to watch for links created to a particular website, such as your personal blog or a campaign landing page. Use the "Link:" syntax.

- Use "as-it-happens" alerts for your most critical searches, and digests (daily or weekly) for the less-important topics, to avoid being overwhelmed.

- Google allows Boolean operators such as *or,* the minus sign, or the asterisk as a wildcard. Use those to narrow or broaden your search terms as appropriate.

The Google Alerts feature brings real-time events and activities to you, providing the chance to analyze them as opportunities for offense or defense. Often, they can provide an additional element: surprise.

For example, as the brand executive owner of a large product at a large company, my name is occasionally referenced on blogs or elsewhere in the context of commentary about certain IBM products or solutions. This usually triggers a Google alert, bringing me to far-flung corners of the Internet to visit bloggers with firsthand experiences and thoughts. Sometimes, I leave a comment simply to indicate to the author that he or she has been heard. It may or may not be possible to act on the content provided, but it builds goodwill to acknowledge their voice and perspective.

Limitations apply as to the effectiveness of Google Alerts in finding relevant new content on the Internet. Sometimes Google's engine doesn't discover and index new Internet content quickly enough. Sometimes alerts arrive 48 hours after a web page has been published, making the information less timely or useful. Also, Google's search crawlers, which scan the Internet for content to index, sometimes don't have access to the websites where your product is being mentioned. This could be the case if, for example, the discussion is in a private password-protected forum.

LinkedIn

LinkedIn is best known for its primary usage, as a business networking site. LinkedIn has replaced the Rolodex or business card file as the way to maintain connections with contacts, colleagues, and even friends and neighbors. It is an online biography and resumé, the encapsulation of digital reputation. Almost all of IBM's employees—more than 325,000—have populated LinkedIn profiles, though there has been no corporate directive to do so.

In some markets or industries, LinkedIn's forums are active, on-topic interactions within an affinity-based group. LinkedIn also provides LinkedIn Answers, a free-form question and answer service. Both methods of discussion on LinkedIn are of high value, as the postings are 100 percent reputation based. Every post is tied to the author's real name and provides single-click access to their background. The lack of anonymity encourages authentic voice.

LinkedIn discussions are more likely to relate to marketplace aspects of your product or service than anywhere else. Active users of LinkedIn are either jobseekers looking to understand types of opportunities in a given market, or they are power networkers, consultants, or others who make a living through reputation. Both seekers and networkers use LinkedIn to build personal brand. Asking intelligent questions or providing insightful answers in community discussions is one way to improve credibility.

However, I find LinkedIn to be the place where the voice of the vendor is least likely to be welcome. On occasion, I have participated in a discussion about our product strategy, market position, or roadmap, with limited traction. Perhaps this is unique to the high-tech software industry, but it does suggest that LinkedIn may be a better tool for active listening to the market than for dialogue.

LinkedIn Answers provides a great way to network through shared interests. In 2008, Danny Mittleman, a professor at Chicago's DePaul University, used LinkedIn Answers to locate a speaker for his class titled Virtual Collaboration. He explicitly asked for someone with Lotus Notes expertise. A day later, I found his question and was able to offer myself up as a speaker. Because my response automatically included my LinkedIn profile, Professor Mittleman knew instantly that I was qualified to speak to his class. To further establish my credentials, I mentioned in my reply that I had previously spoken in another DePaul University classroom (see Figure 7.2). A few weeks later, I lectured in Professor Mittleman's class. The experience became more memorable because each student blogged as part of a classroom assignment—and my Google Alerts picked up their blog entries in the subsequent days.

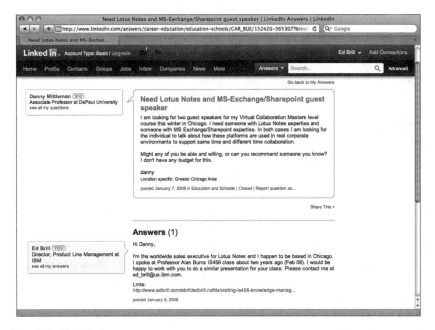

Figure 7.2 LinkedIn Answers.

LinkedIn provides relatively limited tools to monitor group discussion forums or LinkedIn Answers. Some RSS (Really Simple Syndication) feeds, which provide a subscription model for updated links available directly in your web browser, are available. For the most part, though, finding new discussions on LinkedIn is best done through daily or weekly newsletter updates, which the service will send you automatically, or simply allocating some time to participate.

Twitter

The topic of using Twitter as an inbound source is likely already familiar to you. Twitter's equalized ability for anyone to share thoughts in 140 characters results in tweets on almost any topic—from customers, prospects, reporters, analysts, pundits, and competitors.

The voice of the customer likely comes through most strongly on Twitter. Unlike participation in other affinity-based services, or those where real identity is required to participate, Twitter lets anyone say anything. The question for the social product manager is, how important is any one particular tweet?

Some organizations, typically in consumer products or services markets, have deployed community managers to monitor Twitter mentions or respond to inbound tweets directed to their company, brand, or product. The community manager typically functions in a similar organizational role to a customer support manager, measured by their output and responsiveness. However, the community manager is not typically also a business owner. They may or may not be directly connected to the right audience within their organization to channel Twitter feedback.

During the writing of this book, I took a flight on US Airways from their hub in Charlotte, North Carolina. The flight was posted as departing from gate E16A, except that there was no such gate in the airport, nor even a monitor near gate E16 that advertised the flight. In frustration, I tweeted to @USAirways, complaining about the lack of signage and information available in the airport. After asking me to follow them so that they could send me a direct Twitter message, @USAirways sent an extremely unhelpful response telling me that "codeshare flights depart from the A or B concourse."

@USAirways heard nothing further from me. From their point of view, they provided a response, thus their customer relationship management tracking probably considered the interaction closed and complete. Unfortunately for them, all it did was convince me that I would receive nothing valuable out of interacting with US Airways through Twitter. The slight damage to their brand might not have meant much, but as someone who routinely flies more than 100,000 miles per year, this negative interaction shaped my perception of their brand and airline.

As such, I believe there are more risks than benefits to trying to respond to every relevant tweet connected to your product or service. Assessing and validating the importance and relevance of both the content of a tweet as well as the potential influence of the author is an important situation analysis before deciding to respond. Many negative tweets, like anyone's venting of frustration, merit no response. Like Bynkii in Chapter 5, "Picking a Fight," they are not interested in making the product better. Responding only validates their negative position and will likely continue the conversation in that direction.

For my product, a community of advocates—made up of many IBM customers and partners, including some of the IBM Champions (as discussed in Chapter 6, "Activate Your Advocates")—endeavors to answer some of these frustrated tweets. I find this to be admirable and perhaps even more credible than having the vendor do the responding. Humans want to do business with other humans, and the authority that comes from a response generated by a Twitter user whose profile says "IBM Champion" is automatically greater. It is still not clear to what degree these responses help improve perceptions or create positive energy, but at least the person who first tweeted about the product will feel like someone has heard them.

Having said all that, inbound Twitter has a few key uses for the social product manager. The first is as a trend analysis tool. If you make clothing, and the words *broken zipper* keep showing up with your brand name, it is likely an early warning system that one of your products has a quality-control issue. Traditionally, it would take days or weeks for that information to filter up to the vendor, through returns coming in to retailers. Now, direct feedback is available instantaneously, from the end-customer themselves.

Another use for inbound Twitter relates back to Chapter 3, "Self, Product, or Company." Twitter is an important place for social product managers to use their real name and personal brand. Later in this chapter, the notion of outbound messaging through Twitter is discussed, and there it is important for the product manager to be able to demonstrate unique voice versus marketing-oriented tweets. This is also true on inbound. I regularly receive tweets from customers in similar fashion to email, asking specific questions of features or capabilities. Advocates often add me to Twitter discussions that they think might be relevant to me or to a product in IBM's software line.

Receiving a tweet directed at me, or being brought in mid-conversation, provides an opportunity to find the original question or concern and help address it. This human-guided interaction on Twitter is usually much higher value than simply searching for keywords, and my goal is to respond to 75 percent or more of the tweets directed to me. The individual return on investment may be low, but it sends a message to the market around engagement and accessibility. For every 20 tweets I receive that are of limited or no value, the 21st will be a relevant customer interaction or opportunity. That provides the payoff.

Several tools available in the market help make inbound Twitter a more manageable social network. The most useful is a dashboard tool called HootSuite. HootSuite provides a way to track and manage Twitter mentions or keywords. It can analyze trends and topics, providing a filter to narrow attention to content that matters.

The social product manager can benefit from responding to or assisting with the following kinds of inbound messages on Twitter:

- **Traffic cop:** Help customers find their way to the right websites, email addresses, or phone numbers for your organization. A tool like HootSuite holds draft messages that can be used to respond to these kinds of inquiries.

- **Introductions:** Often, contact is initiated via Twitter because the originator has no other way to connect with you. Feel free to respond with your email address, or if you are worried about potential spam or misuse of email, a contact form. Occasionally, you will be asked to follow someone so that he or she can direct message you on Twitter. "Follow back" seems less useful because the person might not otherwise be someone worth following. Use traditional email systems for asynchronous messages instead.

- **Simple queries:** When is a new product coming out? Does your product have a particular capability? These quick questions may be worth a response. It may be especially useful to view these as opportunities for outbound communication. Instead of simply replying to the originator, I often add a dot or the word *hey* in front of such responses, making it a broadcast tweet rather than just a reply to the originator.

Quora

Quora launched in 2010 with a simple mission to be a source for questions and answers. Social product managers can utilize their unique voice to provide authoritative answers on inquiries related to your product or service and build reputation and individual brand in the process.

Quora has added elements of gaming to their service, and linked closely with Facebook or Twitter. Quora also uniquely lets readers nominate someone else to answer a question, when they do not know the answer but instead know someone who would.

During the writing of this book, I have been exploring Quora more often than when it first launched. It seems that the service has taken off in specific industries, such as IT, and in the realm of politics. Otherwise, the volume of questions and answers posted in mainstream topics is relatively limited. Even Coca-Cola, the world's most recognized brand, is receiving only an average of one or two questions per day.

For now, social product managers can benefit from teaming with their community managers and marketing teams to establish an owned presence on Quora. Quora provides excellent notification and monitoring tools, such that it will alert you to any discussion of your product or service in near real time. As an engine, Quora has the most sophisticated question/answer infrastructure of any public social networking tool, and therefore I expect its use will broaden and grow, or it will be absorbed into another social networking environment where the platform can be more broadly adopted.

There are other inbound social networks worth watching, including various geographic tools. In Germany, networking site Xing is as popular as LinkedIn; in Asia, several Twitter-like broadcast environments exist. Social networks such as Pinterest, Digg, and Reddit may have value as inbound tools for your product or industry. Tools which are topic or industry-specific are just as important as the horizontal, public social networks. There are too many of these to adequately cover them in the confines of this book. I encourage you to seek these out for your industry or profession.

Outbound Social Networking Tools

Outbound use of social networking serves a dramatically different purpose than monitoring inbound social media. Outbound is a tool for delivering your content, sending your messages, and shaping your product and personal brands. Outbound social networking requires consideration in the context of marketing campaigns, situation analysis, timing, and amplification.

Outbound social networking is also a place to be relentlessly boring. The "rule of seven"—a marketing truism that a message must be repeated seven times before a prospect absorbs it—applies. Don't be afraid to repeat yourself, within reason. It feels unnatural, but not everyone is tuned in every time and everywhere you post a message.

A key decision in outbound social networking is whether to repeat yourself across multiple networks. Do you need to post the same thing across Twitter, Facebook, LinkedIn, and Google Plus? Or is the specific thought you have at the moment one that fits best in just one of those places? Are you looking to broadcast or converse? Your choice of network may affect your response rate; while writing *Opting In,* I have found that my best response rate is on my personal Facebook profile. At other times, Twitter or blogging have generated greater interaction.

Another consideration for outbound social networking is how much to let your individual personality be part of the communication. As discussed in

Chapter 3, people want to do business with other humans whom they trust. Letting a bit of your own personality through may be useful, depending on your product, industry, and audience, to build a more personal relationship with your online audience.

Determining which tool to use at which time is largely art, and one that is honed over time and with experience. These pointers should help in shaping your perspective on which network serves what purpose at what time.

Blogging

Many of the examples in this book come from my blog. In part, this is due to the maturity of the medium; I started EdBrill.com over a decade ago. A blog is a great place to share structured content, away from the free-for-all of public social networks.

Blogging is a useful format for the following types of messages:

- **Long time horizon:** Blog entries typically stay online and searchable for months or years. A message worth saving fits well on a blog, unlike the highly perishable update format of Twitter or Facebook.

- **Formal words and meaning:** Blog entries are more like writing website content; the words themselves carry weight. For a message intended as an announcement or position statement, a blog is a great tool.

- **Deeper insight:** Because blog entries are typically several paragraphs long, blogging is the best tool to use to go deep on a topic and share your complete point of view.

- **Thought-out responses:** Microblogs typically provoke immediate, simple, gut-reaction responses. Blog entries may have a multiday lifecycle, and so provide the time needed for readers to put additional thought into their responses.

Blogs have the additional benefit of being able to be amplified through other outbound social networking tools. Routinely today, when there is a new blog entry on EdBrill.com, I link to it from Twitter, my Facebook fan page, and my Google Plus profile. Each of those shared links may spawn additional conversation, perhaps even within those social networks, but the core entry continues to deliver its message to new readers.

Blogging has some downsides. The asynchronous nature means that conversations may take place on your blog when it is otherwise relatively dormant. The permanency of most blogs means that updated product roadmaps and positions may be in conflict with earlier public positions. Blogs, especially when they are resident on your company's website, may be taken as official statements, even if they are disclaimed as individual positions. They might also be viewed as tools of your marketing organization, rather than speaking with authentic, unique voice.

The location of a blog is an important decision. A corporate blog is often perceived as marketing speak, but a personal blog is often viewed as less authoritative. I started EdBrill.com as its own site at a time when IBM.com offered no infrastructure for blogging. Today, if I were starting it all over again, either the public IBM Connections implementation on our website or a mainstream blogging tool like WordPress would be the right tool for a new blog. Maintaining one's own website is a long-term commitment to building audience and engagement, both of which can be more easily addressed today by placing the blog on an existing property. Further, use of standardized tools such as WordPress means less site design and maintenance; as new browsers, devices, and networks come along, a blogging platform likely will provide updates to utilize those advancements.

Twitter

Considered the most ubiquitous outbound social network, Twitter also must be considered in light of the potential "signal-to-noise" ratio. Will your message be heard among thousands of tweets per second?

For the social product manager, Twitter is a useful outbound tool for providing timely updates on new products and services, recent updates and releases, and pointers to useful web content—on your own website or others' sites. An ideal mindset is that of a guide, providing the reader with some information of your own along with pointers to other places to turn for additional detail.

Twitter is definitely a medium where it is necessary to decide how much of yourself is part of the message. Many Twitter users choose to segment their messages into multiple IDs, much like the distinction between work and personal email addresses. Tweeting on diverse topics is a quick way to build a larger following; but if your audience needs to filter various interests, they might simply filter you out.

I have struggled with diversity of readership on Twitter since its inception. There are three distinct personalities on a single Twitter ID: my corporate identity at IBM, hometown views, and individual interests such as hobbies or travel.

All of these audiences combined have increased my follower count but, it seems, at a cost of engagement. My tweets are more likely to be retweeted, especially in a business context, than replied to.

A question to be answered in the coming months is whether my experience is common or unique. There seems to be so much content on Twitter today that much of it is getting lost, or having less of an impact than it did when the service was first launched. So, my primary view of Twitter outbound today is the guiding role, with less-unique voice actually delivered via Twitter itself.

However, there are other outbound uses for Twitter, and you might choose to utilize it as an outbound tool for more specific purposes.

Twitter is a great starting-level social network for outbound communication. It is relatively effortless to start using Twitter as a shared bookmark service, tweeting links to useful online articles and information. If you start to do so on a particular range of topics, and apply the right hashtags—keywords flagged with a # as a way to quickly search a topic—you will start to build an audience, and a reputation, related to that topic. This is a solid approach to defining your initial online presence.

Another lightweight approach to engaging on Twitter is event-driven tweets. Most conferences or online events, in any industry, today have a hashtag or Twitter ID that is being used as a common flag for tweets originating from the event. Real-time tweeting from an event will help identify your presence and interests at that event, and likely lead to serendipitous connections, both online and offline.

Facebook

Facebook is considered an ideal outbound tool, whether business to consumer or business to business. Connecting product to prospect or customer requires little commitment, with no ambiguity around individual versus corporate identity. However, use of Facebook in the context of product management requires several considerations.

The first is whether your individual presence on Facebook is related to your work. Do you want to be "friends" with people who simply want to connect because of your product or service? Are you prepared to manage your personal Facebook page in a way that reflects on your product? In many cases, the answer to these should be no, but there are certainly industries or geographies where it is appropriate to connect on an individual level.

For example, after establishing a profile on the service, I started by accepting many Facebook friend requests. I never wanted a prospective customer to feel turned away from IBM because their friend request was declined. However, I quickly recognized that it was important to firewall my personal life online from my professional life. Although I still have many friends on Facebook who are people I work with, I apply Facebook's "do you know this person outside of Facebook?" question as a filter. Remember that building relationships for influence with customers, prospects, and colleagues is important, so tuning out new contacts is a conscious decision to skip Facebook as a networking resource.

There is another option. Facebook pages are the ideal tool for the social product manager. A Facebook page (facebook.com/pages) can be created for your product/service, or for you individually, much like a Twitter ID. The page offers a superior approach to connecting with your marketplace; pages are public, so anyone can find them. A single "like" will bring your page's content even closer to the right audience.

Facebook pages are recognized as a commercial presence on the service, so participant expectations are set appropriately as to the type of interaction that takes place. They offer all the same features as individual profiles, including events, photos, videos, and status updates. You can even use other parts of Facebook as your page's persona so that the page personality can generate likes and other feedback.

Facebook pages can be used for the same outbound communication types as Twitter and other tools, but has the twist of being somewhat more social. Other Facebook users can see who likes your page or your posts, can share them on their own profiles or pages, and can comment and interact with others discussing them.

The Facebook page for Ed Brill, IBM product executive, has attracted several hundred likes. As a positive validation of the effort, more than half of them are people whom I am not friends with on the service. Like Twitter, the Facebook page serves as a broadcast medium with interactivity. I endeavor to respond to comments there and encourage readers to converse with each other as well as with me (see Figure 7.3).

One downside of Facebook pages is reach. Two factors are at play.

First, in order to like a page, customers or prospects must have a Facebook account of their own. The typical Facebook account settings mean that all their friends will see their likes, so they must be comfortable connecting their name to the act of liking your page.

Figure 7.3   Ed Brill persona page on Facebook: www.facebook.com/edbrilldotcom.

Second, your outbound messages may not connect with your audience. Facebook's news feed algorithm, which is sometimes called EdgeRank, means that your page's posts will only display in the feed of *some* of the people who like the page. Third-party optimization tools such as PageLever can help maximize your Facebook reach, and of course, any individual post can be advertised or otherwise promoted to be visible to a broader audience. In fact, such promotional tools on Facebook almost guarantee broader reach, with a high response rate based on being able to very finely choose audience parameters.

If you choose to utilize a Facebook page, be sure to monitor the results of your postings. Facebook will tell you the number of viewers a particular entry has received. If you are hitting the mark, the majority of your fans will see your posts in their status update pages. If not, it is time to evaluate the type of content being posted and how relevant it is to the typical Facebook user.

SlideShare

SlideShare.net does exactly what the name implies: shares your presentations with a public audience, the same way YouTube shares videos. SlideShare today attracts 60 million visitors and 140 million page views per month.

SlideShare's ubiquity, ease of navigation, and mobile device optimization make it a useful tool for reaching a broad audience. For example, in a typical year, I reach at least 10,000 people directly through presentations at conferences and user groups. Posting the same presentation on SlideShare will attract twice that many viewers over the same time period. Many of those will be people I would never otherwise reach, who might not even know any other way to obtain that content from IBM. SlideShare also offers advanced features such as online meetings for broadcasting presentation content, and a lead capture mechanism for "pro" users (see Figure 7.4).

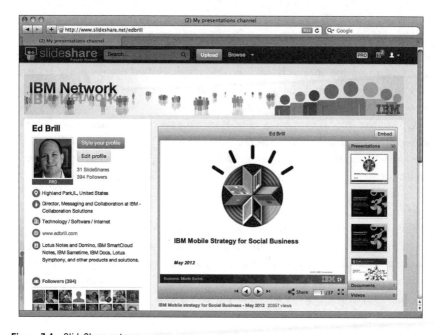

Figure 7.4 SlideShare.net.

One of the very first presentations I posted on SlideShare truly demonstrated the effectiveness of this social network. In 2006, I uploaded a presentation on the "business aspects of social software and collaboration," which had been delivered at a Canadian IT conference. For the next several years, SlideShare users who viewed that presentation—which they often located through keyword (versus author) search—often wanted to know more about IBM's social business story. One such contact invited me to keynote a student event focused on careers in IT at Bowling Green State University in Ohio, solely because of my SlideShare content. Opting in to that event, which provided an opportunity to interact with students and demonstrate how their skills would apply in the work force, was very rewarding.

Other Outbound Mass-Market Tools

There are additional social business tools for effective communication of your messages. These include podcasts, which exist today in many market segments and community interest areas; YouTube, for products or industries where video-based content can add value to the conversation; Google+, which seems to have traction as a more free-form social network in the technology industry; and FourSquare, a location-based service that provides user-to-user tips and recommendations on businesses, restaurants, and activities. Many of the same methods and techniques described earlier aptly transfer over to these additional channels, which can help increase the volume on your message until it is relentlessly boring.

One of the important points of relevance for these mass-market tools is the social product manager as guide or curator. YouTube, for example, isn't a particularly social site; you aren't likely to pick up significant insights as a product manager from the comments left on a video. However, your outbound audience will appreciate links to new YouTube videos produced by your marketing department.

Envisage your role as not solely being about your unique voice but also about your unique perspective in how you view other content. This applies to all the outbound tools, but it is especially important when linking. A simple link tweet prefaced by "Reading:" conveys to your audience that you find the linked material interesting and relevant enough to share.

Forums and Feedback Sites

In addition to the horizontal inbound and outbound tools described previously, a number of sites are designed for more-specific feedback about a product or service. Some of these are appropriate tools for the social product manager to achieve ubiquity, whereas others are best left to marketing and community manager efforts to reach the broad market.

In the past year or two, it seems like every Internet commerce site has integrated social into their business process. Going to a concert? Ticketmaster will link with your Facebook profile and tell you whether any of your friends will be there, right down to where they are sitting. Enjoy a nice meal? OpenTable lets you provide either public or private feedback on the restaurant, shareable globally with just one additional click. Love those new shoes from Zappos? Tell the next potential buyer that they fit just right and were comfortable.

Some Internet commerce sites demand participation without question. A restaurant proprietor must monitor feedback on Yelp, OpenTable, Fork.ly, Foodspotting, and even TripAdvisor. A hotelier must monitor TripAdvisor, Hotels.com, Orbitz, Expedia, Travelocity, Booking.com, Venere, and many other websites. The product managers for airline and hotel loyalty programs are without a doubt reading the forums on FlyerTalk.

All of these channels are obvious sources for inbound feedback. The question is, should the social product manager use them outbound as well?

In most cases, the answer is no. The lessons of Chapter 4, "Offense or Defense," and Chapter 5 apply to all of these interactive discussion and feedback forums. Picking a fight might be useful, or it might provide an opportune channel to play offense or defense. However, vendor participation directly in the discussion can often have a muting effect on authentic voice. Consumers won't provide feedback on a hotel on TripAdvisor if they fear their next check-in at the property will find them blacklisted in some way. Arguing with a bad product review on Amazon.com runs the risk that other consumers will jump in with their own negative experiences.

Forums and interactive feedback sites clearly contribute significant value as authentic voice-of-the-customer reports on real-world use of a product or service. I encourage you to make sure that your customers can find their way to an online service or community where they can share their views freely on how much they like or don't like your product. Leave them to discuss their opinions and findings with like-minded individuals, and the seeds of community will sprout. In the next chapter, I discuss how to take those seeds and make them grow—online or in real life.

Lessons Learned

- The social product manager can effectively utilize the digital grapevine to obtain market feedback directly from customers.
- Social networks provide key vehicles to engage with the market, on both an inbound and outbound basis.
- Key tools include Google Alerts, Facebook, Twitter, and LinkedIn.

Endnotes

[1] IBM, 2011, "From Stretched to Strengthened: Insights from the Global Chief Marketing Officer Study" (www.ibmcmostudy.com).

8

In Real Life

Want to prepare for a career in politics? Try product management.

Shaking hands and making eye contact with customers and prospects is critical real-world campaigning for the social product manager. Typically, these interactions come with an expectation to meet or exceed the customer's requirements in a timely manner.

Thus far, *Opting In* has focused on social business tools as the approach to connecting with the marketplace. However, in this chapter, the lessons learned come from the real world. Meatspace, what Internet users adoringly call real life (as opposed to cyberspace), is an important component of the social product manager's ability to achieve. The examples here showcase face-to-face interactions with organizations and activities that are valuable extensions to the product manager's reach.

You can't hide behind your keyboard all day; talking to live humans is a critical ingredient of the recipe for success.

There are three ways that real world activities can complement online interactions: 1) to amplify your messages; 2) to encourage development of communities and individual relationships; and 3) to broaden networks, and even make friends. Offering to be available for in-person meetings, events, speaking engagements, phone calls, or emails communicates a willingness to carry your message anywhere it needs to go.

Amplify Your Message

Online efforts to reach your customers and prospects will only touch certain segments of the market. The people you need to reach may or may not be able to "hear" you through social media.

One of the frequently asked questions from organizations exploring investments in social business is, what is the payback? An answer can be found in the way that social networking leads to real world interactions and activities.

Being reachable is critical. Gone are the days where a client or prospect would look at a product's data sheet and call the toll-free 1-800 number listed for more information on an offering. Instead, social product managers are responsible for making themselves available through a variety of methods and on a wide spectrum of social sites.

For example, my email address is available in IBM's online corporate directory, published as a link on the home page of my blog, and almost anyone on LinkedIn or Facebook can send me a message. Although it is an elective choice, I crave the connection to the market.

As a product manager, I'm often asked to consult with specific clients. For example, an IT professional may have seen presentations on SlideShare or my blog and want to expose a broader, or more senior, audience in their organization to the same message. Attendees at a conference presentation might want to have the same message carried to another venue. Even the customer I met directly months ago may reconnect to obtain an update on the latest strategy or product plans.

The common thread through all of these is being approachable. Building a digital reputation of being engaged, transparent, and genuine encourages those you encounter online to consider you as a trustworthy resource. Opportunities to amplify your message will present themselves as a result. It might feel a little like political activity, and you are doing a bit of selling yourself, as described in Chapter 3, "Self, Product, or Company," but the results will remove any queasy feeling quickly.

One method of melding meatspace and social networks is advertising availability. Customers and prospects may not realize that you actually *want* to talk to them! Whether in person or through e-meetings, telling your social network followers that you are willing to be part of direct interactions will lead to increased engagement and amplification.

I travel all over the world to meet my customers, and there are times when more meetings can be accommodated during a trip. If I have a free block of time, advertising that availability—what I call availablogging[1]—often leads to additional opportunities for useful face-to-face interaction.

For example, a few years ago I traveled to Switzerland for a business meeting. I planned to walk off jet lag and answer emails upon arrival. As a result of communicating my trip plans through my blog, instead I ended up in three customer meetings between Zurich and Bern.

The Swiss meetings were arranged by tapping into my social network of business partners, thereby providing an opportunity to reach additional clients. Three additional and useful conversations materialized, all of which helped both the customer's and my own objectives.

Once you are participating in successful real-world networking, a multiplier effect kicks in quickly. The Swiss business partner tells other partners and customers that I was a useful asset in working with his customers; suddenly, requests for my time come in from Austria and Germany. A return invitation to Zurich materializes to speak at a local technology user group.

The business cards I pass out in these meetings extend the multiplier even further (see Figure 8.1). While anyone can find me online, the real estate of my cards encourages that engagement.

More than the specifics of how to locate profiles or websites, the business card carries a message: Let's connect! It builds additional credibility that you want to be part of the conversation.

My business card lists three websites that are intended to be invitations. None of these websites are run by IBM, but they represent ways to be part of the extended IBM community. For example, OpenNTF.org is an open source community for application developers who work with Lotus Notes; this community was born through social business and has been growing for more than a decade. I discuss OpenNTF more in the next section of this chapter.

Figure 8.1   Business card.

Develop Community and Individual Relationships

Community is a core principle of social business. Formation of communities around shared interests continues to be one of the building blocks of the Internet today. The example inbound social business tools in Chapter 7, "Tools of the Trade," highlight ways to engage and leverage aggregation of like-minded individuals.

The social product manager as leader has the opportunity to sow the seeds of these communities, through validation and contribution. A single tweet or blog entry of "link love" directed at a community website accomplishes two things: 1) curation, providing a guide to your followers to lead them to others with similar interests; and 2) endorsement, lending the product manager's authority and confidence to the content and fabric of the community.

In crossing from virtual to physical worlds, the product manager can likewise sanction a community by participating in face-to-face events. Communities of enthusiasts like to meet in real life. For example, Mini Cooper owners love to drive road rallies together. Apple fans hang out in the Apple store, whether they are making purchases that day or not, and share tips onsite in small groups. Similarly, communities of IBM software users have energetically formed regional and global user groups, which have presented improved opportunities for community feedback for product managers.

As a whole, the IT industry has shifted from large global-scale conferences to smaller local events, and that transformation has been driven entirely by social business. Years ago, to hear from subject matter experts, IT professionals would have to travel to traditional expensive conferences. Some of those still happen, and they are critical to the support of the market. Through community evolution, smaller user group events have gained in importance.

The user group succeeds because the expertise needed to provide value for the group is more easily identifiable today. Knowledgeable experts participate in online communities, building their digital reputations. Organizers already know who the potential contributors are for an event, based on their contributions and expertise. Because those potential speakers and moderators in turn have online followings, they become a draw for additional potential participants. Birds of a feather flock together, as they say.

The market for live presentation of expert content has democratized as a result. Instead of paying to attend conferences, user groups tend to be run at little or no charge to the attendees. Vendors still pay to exhibit at such events, but that revenue is now typically sufficient to pay for a venue and activities. Speakers often no longer expect to be paid honoraria for sharing their expertise, but rather do so to enhance their digital reputation or to give back to the community.

As a vendor, we have tried to strike a careful balance of influence and expectation with user groups. Too much IBM presence leads to the feel of a marketing event. Too little IBM contribution creates an impression of orphanage. In the name of encouraging community development, IBM often provides one or more speakers to every user group.

The product manager's physical presence at these events serves multiple purposes. First is the endorsement of the event itself; an IBM speaker at one of our user groups lends credibility and draws participation. Second is delivery of our message, often in a more unfiltered way than traditional conferences or events. Third, and probably most important, is to provide a way for the vendor to hear from and build relationships with individuals firsthand, in a more-relaxed setting than a customer briefing or onsite meeting.

Over the past several years, I have utilized user group presentations as a way to test potential future decisions or announcements. Unlike a presentation to a client where an imminent transaction may be on the line, when there is no specific deal on the table it is often easier to speak candidly about thoughts on new features, packaging, product combinations, or competition. The product manager as politician can employ user groups and similar venues as straw polls, confirming or altering planned activities as a result of feedback in the smaller, more intimate setting among typically loyal advocates.

Admittedly, there is some theater to that line of thinking, as well. Occasionally, knowing full well that there are people in the room who are live-tweeting or will otherwise share what they learned at the event, sometimes the user group is a way to see how the community will react to an idea even before it is ready.

For example, in the summer of 2011, I attended a small user group event in Milwaukee. After my presentation was complete, I answered a few questions. In one of them, I revealed a "skunkworks" project—an effort in our labs that was not part of an official product, but rather a simple technical exploration—and measured the feedback from the room as to whether the concept was useful. Because the idea was at that point brand new to the market, a few people quickly shared their enthusiasm on Twitter. The reaction was positive, but more important, sharing new and somewhat raw information indicated to those attending that particular event that it was worthwhile. They received unique content, and the decision to share communicated to them that I had assessed the event's value sufficiently as to deem it a useful place to test this concept. This type of give and take improved relationships with both attendees and event organizers.

Communities can develop with various specialized interests. In computer software, for the last decade or so, it has been popular for application developers to participate in "open source" community efforts. Open source efforts are computer programs where all the programming source is available and anyone can contribute improvements to that source code. An open source community for Lotus Notes developers has existed for some time, and through careful engagement and strong community leadership has grown and flourished over the past decade.

HOW IBM MADE SOFTWARE DEVELOPMENT SOCIAL

Paul Withers, senior developer, Intec Systems Ltd.

Bruce Elgort, president and CEO, Elguji Software

IBM has historically approached software development in a traditional manner: Major and minor product releases were circulated as beta releases to design partners, and subsequently at certain points extended to members of a managed beta program. The approach to product fixes has been equally traditional—fix packs released approximately quarterly, with interim fixes released on an ad hoc basis to address more urgent issues.

But the inclusion of a new development technology, XPages, added a change of pace that required a more agile approach to software development. XPages is an application development platform for programs used through a web browser or on a mobile device. Computer programmers and developers use XPages to build innovative applications focused on helping people to collaborate.

The XPages capability went through the usual design and beta programs for its release. At the same time, though, IBM also engineered an additional library of XPages capabilities, which bypassed the traditional testing process.

The XPages Extension Library was released to all potential consumers at once, instead of first passing through traditional pre-release testing channels. It was released to OpenNTF.org, an independent open source community site. IBM was taking its software in a new social direction.

OpenNTF.org was created in 2001 by Bruce Elgort and Nathan Freeman. At the time, there was no single place on the web for developers to freely share their Lotus Notes applications. OpenNTF has become an integral part in the success of Lotus Notes over the past ten years. Both software and its source code are available on the site, which acts as a community effort and accepts contributions from anyone.

By 2011, OpenNTF evolved from a two-person sharing site into a nonprofit with 31 members organization, along with hundreds of volunteer contributors.

OpenNTF has had a tremendous impact on IBM's software development process. For the new XPages library, bugs and feature requests could be submitted on the OpenNTF community website. IBM's engineers directly addressed the reported issues, on an unusually aggressive schedule. Between September 2010 and December 2011, there were 49 releases of the Extension Library—more than one release every two weeks—driven through the social interactions on the OpenNTF website. IBM also asked the community for prioritization of components to release in the officially supported product, tapping into the wisdom of the crowds.

Documentation also departed from IBM's usual approach. Demonstrations were included in the releases on OpenNTF, to showcase all new functionality in action. Videos were published by IBMers on YouTube. Full documentation of the new features took a traditional approach of a published book, an expected documentation source for software developers but with a social twist. IBM's chief architect used Twitter (https://twitter.com/philriand/status/32730855042457601) to ask for community members to write the book.

The whole software development lifecycle for the XPages Extension Library marked a radical shift by IBM. The software giant was now taking into account the expectations of 21st century developers, who want more than a black box solution handed to them. The approach enabled software development to be handled in a social, open, and agile manner, empowering customers while surrendering some vendor control.

As time went on, IBM and the OpenNTF community introduced many additional applications, including blogging, help desk support, wikis, discussion forums, and hundreds more. In a single month, OpenNTF records between 12,000 and 18,000 downloads. OpenNTF also now hosts educational opportunities and contests, challenging the community of developers to continue their efforts with the motivation of recognition.

As Elgort and Withers describe, OpenNTF.org has become a critical extension of IBM's efforts into the community, without actually being organized or operated by IBM. OpenNTF is both an online and a real-life endeavor, with annual meetings, project meet-ups, and more informal face-to-face interactions among contributors.

Care and feeding of the community participating in OpenNTF is a critical success factor in driving adoption of the technology itself. Many of the projects on OpenNTF offer solutions that can be deployed in any organization, whether or not they use any form of Notes today. Thus, OpenNTF is not only an outlet for developers wanting to contribute to the success of the platform, it is also a source for additional market expansion.

The best sources of market intelligence are individual voices. Although product managers must avoid giving too much weight to the last customer they visited or a single high-profile customer, successful understanding of market requirements often comes one contact at a time.

Being social and engaging with the market online means building relationships, which turn out to be both external and internal. Whether at events, within communities, or individually, having the right contacts with customers and partners often enhances decision making, accelerates innovation and ideation, and activates the market.

One of the challenges for social business is time management. We all need to get work done eventually, and a common criticism of social networking is being spread too thin. When on the road at events or meetings, a balancing act ensues. I find some of my best writing time to be in the relative seclusion of an airplane, even crammed into a middle seat in economy class. I find myself using Facebook more when I am on the road, sharing a bit more on the personal side than when seated in my home office. Twitter use decreases, however, because the event or meeting where I am participating takes most of my real-time attention.

The practice of product management at IBM has evolved substantially over the past 15 years. In the past, it was rare for a product manager to maintain an ongoing relationship with any individual customer. We might see the same faces at a conference or user group, or conduct an annual briefing, but otherwise the interaction was limited.

Now, the individual relationships matter. As IBM's CEO and CMO studies identified, customer intimacy on that individual level is crucial for success. When our design partner program (described in Chapter 6, "Activate Your Advocates") holds an online meeting, there is recognition among the screen names and live video images of who the individuals are and what interests they hold. As a social product manager, I can leverage my relationships with clients, partners, and influencers to enroll participants in an event or speaking engagement. The relationships with key contacts are in place for direct assistance, without passing through IBM's sales organization. When a reference or example from a customer is needed, I can confidently reach out to my network of contacts, knowing that those individuals with whom I have built relationships will be listening and ready to assist.

One of those is Brian O'Neill, a customer who has witnessed IBM's transformation as a social business.

THE CUSTOMER POINT OF VIEW: IBM BECOMING A SOCIAL BUSINESS

Brian O'Neill, social business and collaboration specialist,
W. L. Gore & Associates, Inc.

I began my interactions with IBM as a Lotus Domino customer after accepting a position as a Domino administrator at W. L. Gore & Associates, Inc. (Gore) in September 2001. At the time, I was fairly familiar with the Lotus Notes client, and this was my first interaction with Domino and the large corporation behind them both.

In 2001, Gore employed 6,000 associates. This certainly wasn't tiny from a vendor's point of view, but also not really a huge number that demands major attention. I can remember my first face-to-face meeting with IBM sales. It was described to me by teammates at Gore as a "normal six-month check in" with IBM sales. The meeting was unbalanced—four of us and seven IBMers. It seemed that half the meeting was spent on introductions. The second half of the meeting consisted of those seven IBMers taking a lot of follow-up actions to answer questions. Subsequent meetings went along in a similar fashion, except maybe we spent the first half of these meetings going over the questions we still didn't have answered from the previous meeting. The relationships were good, but the information we needed didn't flow at the pace desired.

Fast forward to now, 2012. Gore has grown in size to nearly 10,000 associates. As before, not tiny and not huge. But my experience working with IBM has changed drastically. Although we still have meetings with IBM Sales and this face-to-face time is still valuable, it's what happens in setting up the meetings that has changed: IBMers have made it known that they use their internal BluePages (commercially known as IBM Connections) to find the right associates to attend our meetings. It's what happens during the meetings: If they don't know the answer, they reach out, in real time, with instant messaging to associates who can give us the answer—right then and there. It's what happens after the meetings: They stay engaged with us via their own Greenhouse, or Twitter, Facebook and Skype. They share information on the IBM website and those run by product managers such as edbrill.com and lbenitez.com. We've even had a product manager make real-time updates on a product support wiki for information we needed about a specific feature. All of this, because IBM is not only selling social business tools, they are encouraging each one of their employees to be social.

In the end, we are a more informed customer better enabled to implement our strategy to support our business.

Make Friends

One aspect of social business that isn't discussed much is the very natural human result of all this engaging, transparent, and agile interaction: developing friendships. Social business is about empowering people. As IBM Vice President Jeff Schick often says, "Social business is about connecting people with information and people with people." The human element of being social significantly drives participation and feedback.

Early in the development of social networking, Forrester Research established a profile of social software adoption. From their research, the vast majority of participants in social networking were spectators—those simply viewing the interactions of others. Joiners and creators were smaller numbers, along with other roles. In other words, not everyone needs to be social to derive value from social.

But among those who are, as relationships form, so do friendships. The whole idea of opting in to social interactions is to involve the human element in communications among employees, customers, partners, and suppliers. Inevitably, snippets of individual personality shine through.

Chapter 3 described the notion of representing yourself as well as your product and company. Sharing interests leads to stronger interest in yourself as an individual, and people like to do business with people they personally like.

Personal sharing does not work for everyone. Some will find that the tradeoffs of privacy versus being social weigh in the direction of holding back. People who hold more senior positions inside an organization must carefully weigh their personal interactions in public, lest a comment be taken out of context or ascribed incorrectly. The same filters you might apply to a business networking event can be your guide to online socialization, at least as a starting point.

The ratio of business to personal sharing matters, too. Different audiences interact for different reasons, but those that follow me online expect primarily to hear about my work at IBM. Overloading them with my personal pursuits may lead to being tuned out or hidden, thus neutralizing my reach and effectiveness as a social product manager. Balance is important, while still recognizing that need to create an individual human identity.

Elements of my personality that are highly visible online include being a foodie—interested in a great meal anytime, traveling the world and exploring, photography, and my hometown of Highland Park, Illinois, where I also live today. All of those have resulted in building friendships or personal relationships beyond the context of my day job itself.

In 2008, on a business trip to Sydney, Australia, I landed quite early on a Sunday and found myself a bit jetlagged from the long voyage. However, one of the weekend pleasures there is a visit to the Rocks Market, an arts and crafts showcase right near Sydney Harbour.

Using Twitter, I announced my presence there. A short time later, a follower named Tony Hollingsworth responded to me with a welcoming message, and proceeded to offer a couple of restaurant recommendations in the neighborhood. That very day, I found myself seated at the common table of Sailor's Thai, one of Hollingsworth's suggestions, tucking into curry and rice.

While grateful for the local recommendation, I didn't think much more of it until a few days later, when presenting at a customer event. I then blogged the following:

> *People sometimes ask me why I think Twitter is so valuable. While we're not directly conducting business on there very often, I do learn a lot through what others are talking about, and it helps me get a clearer picture of names in the industry. One fine example took place at the customer luncheon in Sydney last week. Someone stood up to ask me a question, and he started by telling me that*

he was @hollingsworth on Twitter, who had been giving me restaurant recom-
mendations for the last few days in Sydney. Knowing who he was and that he
was a Twitter user was helpful in answering his question, because it gave me
an opportunity to mention {a new Twitter tool for my product}. Our connection
was immediately stronger despite having never met in-person nor even so much
as heard Tony's name before.[2]

Hollingsworth and I still tweet occasionally, having discovered that he even has a separate Twitter ID (@AskTonyFood) for sharing his love of a good meal. For sure, I know that he can help me have a better travel experience anytime I'm in Australia.

One unintended consequence of being so publicly passionate about food—I have blogged about Michelin three-star dinners and posted customized birthday dinner menus on Facebook—is that it has set a travel expectation that I might only be impressed by a great restaurant. It has taken much expectation resetting for colleagues in Asia to understand that I'd rather eat street food than eat with sterling cutlery, or sample the local oxtail stew in Spain instead of playing it safe with a burger. Still, even this can lead to tighter friendships and working relationships.

In 2010, I visited Chile at the request of an IBM business partner, DyDeCom. They had contacted me through my blog, playing out all the tenets of the previous chapters—their email expressed hope that I was approachable and concerned about IBM customers globally. It turned out this was the first time they had had an IBM executive visit their primary customer, and they felt obligated to make the trip worthwhile. After we concluded our business meetings, we visited some of the Chilean wineries in the Casablanca Valley. The DyDeCom employees themselves had never done this, so teaching them how to taste wines and enjoy the complementary cheeses was a great way to share experiences. After leaving the country, the DyDeCom staff and I remained connected via Twitter and blogs, continuing our work (and our friendship).

Every December, edbrill.com features a "year in review," and among the metrics measured is whether I visited any new countries that year. The opportunity to experience new places and cultures always ranks high on my travel prioritization. In 2007, I was able to squeeze an event taking place in Portugal into my itinerary, my first and thus far only visit to the country. Because of a late arrival, my packed agenda had to be further compressed, and I ended up with little free time. Still, a determined blog reader and sometime online chat contact named Vitor Periera insisted he would find a way for us to connect. When we couldn't spend much time together at the event itself, he offered to give me a lift to the airport—the next morning. I don't know where Periera lived or how far out of the way it was for him or how early he had to wake to give me a lift. I was especially grateful to him, and for the human connection in meatspace, no matter how brief.

A few years later, at an IBM event in Madrid, Vitor Periera appeared again. He had driven all the way from Lisbon—over 400 miles (600 km), including through a bad traffic jam—just to come to the event. Periera didn't even speak Spanish fluently. I learned that he felt more connected to IBM through me than anyone locally. I was touched by his candor and enthusiasm. Periera has since moved to Ireland, and hopefully one day we will have the opportunity to meet there, too.

These human connections are why I also advocate the use of location-based services such as TripIt and FourSquare. While conscious of the privacy concerns these services introduce, the benefit of being able to communicate current or planned location and travel seems to outweigh the risks. Obviously, you must do your own situation analysis to see whether you or your family have any concerns about sharing this type of information online.

TripIt has been an extremely useful tool. The site itself (tripit.com) provides a high-value set of capabilities for the business traveler, all initiated simply by sending travel itineraries to the service over email. TripIt's benefits include consolidation of itineraries into a single access point, the ability to share them across multiple devices, and integration with my blog/Facebook/LinkedIn such that others will know about my upcoming planned trips. Just avoiding the question "What hotel are you staying in tonight?" from family members alone makes the free service valuable. The announcement of upcoming travel is another form of "availablogging," and has led to many positive meetings or connections. When they can see where I will be traveling, readers and followers ask about possible IBM events or other open activities that might provide an opportunity for us to meet.

FourSquare is a location-based service that tells your contacts where you are at any given time. It, too, integrates with Twitter and Facebook; so if you want to be very public about where you are having dinner, you can do that. Typically, FourSquare users have a much smaller network of contacts who can always see their latest location through the service. I use this with a core group of 100 contacts only, people I know and trust enough for them to know when I'm not at home. Those are also the same people with whom I'm most likely to want to connect if we happen to be in the same place at the same time.

One such example was a recent visitor to Chicago—a consultant and IBM business partner—who wanted restaurant recommendations. It turned out the cafe in the hotel where she was staying was highly rated and someplace I had recently tried. I shared the recommendation, and she and her children had a great meal, which I followed on Instagram as she posted photos of their dishes. Indeed, Chapter 3's lessons of self played out in the real world, successfully. That's why I'm always happy to connect on a human level and play virtual tour guide for my hometown. It helps project an online sense of who I am and what I believe in.

Through both TripIt and FourSquare, I routinely connect with my customers, colleagues, and business partners as I travel the world. It might simply be a cup of coffee or it might be an adventure, but the chance to make the real-world connection often pays off. It feels sometimes like a politician, trying to listen to all the voters and constituents, but most of the time, genuine, heartfelt, friendly interaction results.

For the nerdy kid who started his employment history at Burger King, having thousands of friends all over the world as a result of doing a job I enjoy is pretty rewarding. Although I will never seek a real career in politics, every day brings new contacts and opportunities. These experiences are why I love product management.

Lessons Learned

- The social product manager can use real-world interactions to amplify messages and further activate advocates.
- The social product manager can leverage real-world activities and endorsements to influence communities and build individual relationships.
- The social product manager can make friends and have fun connecting people with information and people with people

Endnotes

1 My friend Ben Rose added the term *availablogging* to UrbanDictionary. com. See www.urbandictionary.com/define.php?term=availablogging.

2 Edbrill.com, "New Zealand Herald: IT sellers talk up social links," November 27, 2008 (www.edbrill.com/ebrill/edbrill.nsf/dx/ new-zealand-herald-it-sellers-talk-up-social-links).

9

Social Inside the
Organization

Ken Blanchard, author of *The One Minute Manager,* is widely quoted as saying, "The key to successful leadership today is influence, not authority."

A social business uses both technology and culture to create business value and drive competitive advantage. The entire organization participates, delivering better outcomes in every department, division, and role.

In most companies, the product or brand manager acts as an influence leader, not a direct line manager. Thus, the social product manager can be more successful by using the capabilities of a social business to enhance their influence, stimulating better decisions and results internally.

Until now, *Opting In* has focused on marketplace interaction. Social product managers have been defined primarily in terms of their connections with customers, partners, and suppliers. In this chapter, the focus is inward influence—making the product manager, and the entire organization, more effective through being a social business.

Intersecting Organizational Goals and Social Tools

For the past several years, IBM has published an annual CEO study. Like the CMO study quoted in the previous chapter, the IBM Global CEO study is the result of large-scale interviews of more than 1,700 chief executives across every industry and around the world. The 2012 version of the study recognized three primary themes:

- Empowering employees through values
- Engaging customers as individuals
- Amplifying innovation with partnerships

The notion of engaging customers as individuals is clearly the core principle of *Opting In*. When that engagement model becomes part of the fabric of an organization, it then permeates into the other two themes from the CEO study. Employees who are engaged, transparent, and agile are more productive and influential within an organization as well as outside it.

The CEOs interviewed for the 2012 IBM study recognized the value of using social tools for empowerment:

{W}ith more employees participating in highly social, media-rich environments outside of work, traditional corporate collaboration tools look outdated and limiting. "To connect with the new generation of employees," a banking CEO from Argentina acknowledged, "we will need to change communication methods. We are the email generation; they are the social network generation." ...CEOs are also contemplating different management systems and organizational structures. "In a rapidly changing environment, we must foster free communication and eliminate layers to maintain speed," explained a professional services company CEO from Japan. An insurance CEO from the Caribbean put it more bluntly, "We need to blow up the hierarchy so ideas can flow up more easily."[1]

Social product managers can grow their influence by capturing the voice of the customer (or prospective customer) and using it to relentlessly advocate within the organization. To do so effectively, the organization must adopt a culture of open knowledge sharing, and put in place the tools to ensure effective communication.

In discussing the landmark report "Making the business case for enterprise social networks," Altimeter Group founder Charlene Li describes enterprise social networks (ESN) as "a new way to communicate and form relationships—and because of that, can bridge gaps that exist in terms of information sharing and decision-making processes." Li goes on to describe four organizational challenges that can be addressed through the use of ESNs:

1. "Encourage sharing. Remember how revolutionary email was? It fundamentally changed the way we communicated by reducing the cost/effort and collapsing the time frame and scaling it to include multiple recipients. Social represents a fundamental change, simply because, at its essence, it encourages sharing. The simple presence of a status update box on a page encourages people to share their thoughts, activities, and expertise."
2. "Capture knowledge. Capturing the collective knowledge of an organization is a daunting task because it includes a wide range of facts, information, and skills gained through experience. Yet few people proactively sit down each day to document and capture their knowledge. ESNs provide an opportunity to do just that, by capturing glimpses of knowledge through profiles, activity streams, and interactions."
3. "Enable action. Having an ESN in place means that operations and processes can begin to change as well. This happens when the day-to-day process changes because the ESN enables new relationships and behaviors that address a gap that prevented actions from being taken."
4. "Empower employees. The last way ESNs drive value is that they empower and embolden people to speak up and join together, as well as gives them opportunities to contribute their skills and ideas."[2]

As a 2008 IBM white paper described, cultural change must be the first step in becoming a social business inside the organization:

Companies must make data available to more people in the organization; change the corporate culture to one of collaboration and trust; and implement tools to harness collective knowledge, experience and communities. If companies are successful in these efforts, they can unleash a world of new innovators. They can capitalize on the way many workers—including the next generation of business leaders—already connect. They can prepare themselves for collaborative innovation and the business success that collaboration makes possible.[3]

In other words, corporate culture plus strategy plus tools are the key ingredients for a social business. All three are essential for the recipe to succeed.

IBM as a Social Business

The "Digital IBMer" has become a core competency throughout IBM worldwide. The goal is to focus IBM interactions on concrete outcomes that deliver business value—enhancing social presence, increasing and projecting expertise, engaging with clients, and collaborating to innovate.

Dozens of tools have been deployed, but more important, the entire organization has embraced the concepts behind the tools. All IBM employees have access to training tools as well as to mentors and guides to help them establish *digital eminence*. In her book *Get Bold!*, IBM Vice President Sandy Carter outlined the five ways that IBM has aligned our goals and culture as a social business:

1. Role and guidelines. As discussed previously, the IBM Social Computing Guidelines established a standard of expectation for its employees.
2. Empowerment. IBM encouraged everyone to participate and empowered employees through trust. IBM views its employees as its best brand ambassadors.
3. Educate and enable. IBM has numerous internal online education and in-person education offerings on best practices and tools and techniques in the social realm.
4. Build a culture for participation. IBM tracks the positive return on investment (ROI) and expense reduction that we see from our internal social business footprint. We engage employees in shaping IBM's future through internal social tools, both ongoing and at a moment in time.
5. Experiment and have a way to learn from mistakes. IBM has set up social business digital councils in several divisions to share ideas, collect best practices, and learn from mistakes.[4]

As a technology company, the cultural change at IBM was driven simultaneously while adopting collaborative tools. For example, corporate instant messaging, through our own IBM Sametime product, was never formally rolled out. It was simply adopted virally, as employees found that their peers were more responsive to a simple "ping" than to emails or voicemails.

That the same tool features one-click conversion from conversation drove increased utilization of e-meetings. Once those tools became acceptable culturally, as a company we were able to adopt a policy change: Travel for internal meetings is only by rare exception. Today, more than 50 million instant messages are sent within IBM per day, and 49 million minutes of e-meetings are conducted each month, a significant improvement in organizational efficiency.

Other social sharing apps likewise accelerated flattening the organization, especially after the 2005 introduction of the IBM Social Computing Guidelines. For example, although IBM's intranet had provided the ability to share files—that is, posting a presentation, spreadsheet, document, or image such that other IBMers could access them—for several years, a research project that included a self-service mechanism for file sharing changed the internal culture quickly. Anyone could post content, such as customer-ready presentations, making them accessible to any other part of the organization. Anyone looking for content on a specific topic could search for relevant files based on keywords or tags. At the same time, anyone and everyone could see the number of downloads for a specific file, which people had downloaded the file, and whether people had recommended it or commented on it. Organization-wide search and sharing made content available around the globe, from every level in the organization. Content was now crowdsourced and always up-to-date.

The result: More than 750,000 files have been shared—resulting in 22 million downloads. That is a lot of self-service empowerment. As a product manager, I no longer field regular questions asking for my latest customer-facing roadmap or strategy presentations. They are simply available on "my files," for any IBMer to access, anytime.

This file sharing capability was born of necessity within IBM, but eventually became invention as part of a product, IBM Connections, that we sell today. It became so useful we also made it available in a cloud computing model, on IBM's SmartCloud, so we could use the same engine to share content with customers, partners, and suppliers, in the same social engagement manner.

At IBM, social capabilities are embedded into many additional horizontal and departmental applications, thereby helping the Digital IBMer make sense of the content itself. For example, the foundational element of IBM's internal social platform is the employee profile, which started out as an application called BluePages. Unlike traditional corporate directory applications, an employee himself or herself provides most of the information in the profile. Static information may include their background or resumé, academic accomplishments, and languages spoken. Variable components of the profile can include current projects, availability, and mentoring activity. IBM's human resources system populates elements of the profile, as well, including location, contact information, and reporting hierarchy.

Interestingly, though, one field that is self-defined on an IBM employee's profile is the employee's job title. Standardized position descriptions may be too narrow or too generic to identify individual areas of responsibility, so we empower employees to define themselves in the eyes of other IBMers. That permission extends to more creative elements of the profile such as the employee's photo. The human element is a choice, and provides another layer for contributing to one's own digital reputation.

Through the various elements of self-definition in an employee's profile, along with features like tagging, where other users apply labels to people based on their expertise, a much more complete picture of that individual emerges. Within IBM, this information is then analyzed by an internal expertise locator. Instead of having to ask managers or peers for help locating the appropriate IBM resource for information or skills, social tools provide the guidance to discover what the organization already knows, and who knows it. This is an area where we continue to conduct research and internal innovation, which should lead to improved precision in locating knowledge and expertise throughout the organization (see Figure 9.1).

Other social tools are available to every IBMer, including the following:

- **Blogs and microblogs**: More than 30,000 IBMers write internal blogs, and many more utilize a microblogging tool for small, fast updates. Internal microblogging has established itself as a key team communication vehicle for personal status, or what the social web has begun to call "narrating your work" or "working out loud." Instead of emailing my staff to tell them when I am going to be out of the office, I post a microblog entry indicating location, activity, and availability. This makes for more efficient communication as the phrase "I don't know where he is or when I can get in contact with him" has been left behind.

  This has become an especially useful concept in an organization where staff are geographically dispersed around the world. My own work teams are typically hundreds or thousands of miles away from me. We may meet face to face only a few times a year. The microblog provides a window into "my office," since nobody can walk down the hallway to check on my whereabouts.

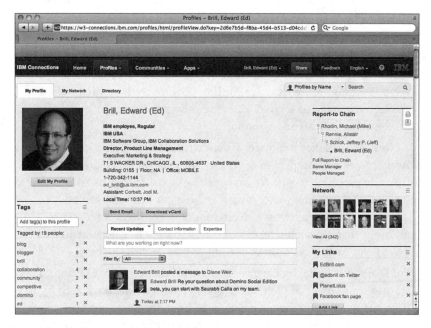

Figure 9.1   IBM Connections profile.

Blogs, both in written and audio/video form, have replaced a wide variety of broadcast communications that used to take place over email. Executive communications have an extended reach and life span, with much more leading by example. Information in blogs can be discussed and improved. Ideas can be generated and supported through special ideation blogs. In short, blogs have moved the culture inside IBM from sending to sharing.

- **Wikis**: 75,000 unstructured self-service websites exist on the IBM intranet, with more than 60 million page views since the service began in 2007.

- **Communities**: Thousands of online communities of interest have been defined within IBM. These include project-oriented teams, departments, disciplines, and shared interests. For example, the Mac @ IBM community has thousands of members. Those using Apple Mac desktops at IBM, myself included, use the community to provide peer-level assistance on software tools, configuration issues, product reviews, and workarounds. Intriguingly, in the three years that I have used a Mac desktop within IBM, I have never called our internal help desk for assistance with it—primarily because the Mac community typically holds the answers to my questions.

- **Bookmarks**: A bookmark sharing service replaces the old approach of emailing links to interesting web content, fostering a culture of sharing versus sending. More than 1.5 million bookmarks have been shared through the internal service, allowing others to comment on particular content and indicate its usefulness.

- **Activities:** Another tool used widely within IBM is called Activities. Activity-centric computing organizes work around the objective, rather than the process or tools. An activity tracks structured and unstructured information around a project, such as meeting minutes, to-dos, documents, and interactions. Activities are organized as templates, meaning that repeatable processes can be themselves documented as knowledge assets, carrying over from one project to the next.

  For *Opting In*, activities have been an invaluable tool. In addition to storing the content of each of the book's chapters, the book activity has been the production management hub. Contributions, permissions, artwork, templates, front matter, and reviewer input have all come together in the activity. As other IBMers have joined on to the effort to produce this book, a single self-service action is all that is needed to add them as readers or editors to the activity. The entire process is logically organized and could be applied again as a template to any other book's creation (see Figure 9.2).

In addition, many project-specific or community-specific social apps are in use within IBM today. For example, one community, Generation Open (GenO), is built around social business tools, processes, and management systems. GenO creates instant communities of global teams to collaborate on projects and products. Project managers, team leaders, consultants, and IT architects post projects; people who are in-between assignments or have free time opt in to these projects to add their talents and expand their skills.

GenO reduces the time it would have taken to complete projects by 30 percent, increases the reuse of "software assets" by 50 percent, and cuts component costs by 33 percent.

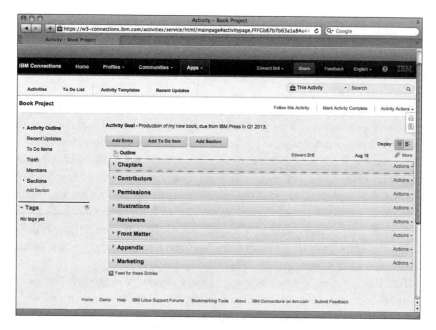

Figure 9.2 Example of an IBM Connections activity.

IBM's use of social business tools isn't limited to employees sitting at their desks. Smartphones and tablets are just as important to our internal connections. IBM's adoption of a "bring your own device" (BYOD) policy, which allows any employee to connect his or her personal phone or tablet to IBM network resources, has extended the reach of these social tools to mobile employees and home offices. IBM was already a leader in empowering a mobile work force—half of IBM's employees in the United States, for example, have no permanent office assignment. BYOD, combined with a culture already attuned to distributed work, plus social tools, equals a highly engaged culture of sharing: anytime, anywhere.

Many of the social tools used by IBMers have native application interfaces on iPhone, iPad, Android, and BlackBerry devices. Using my iPhone and iPad, I can easily address any computing requirements while traveling away from the office. Presentations can be delivered directly from the iPad, which also has the ability to access updated content on-the-fly if needed. Videos, white papers, and other collateral tools are all also available within IBM's social libraries available through iPad applications.

It's been my experience that customers seem somewhat surprised when an IBM executive attends an in-person meeting with only a tablet device, fully productive. I predict that in a few years, though, this will be a norm as the worldwide mobile work force swells past 1 billion in 2013, according to research firm IDC.[5]

Because all these social tools are available from anywhere globally, the practice of product management at IBM has changed significantly. Product managers are no longer expected to be co-located with their development teams; the engineers themselves are spread out among IBM's global network of lab sites. Many product managers work from home offices or more remote sites, myself included. Digital reputation establishes the leadership needed for my team and me to accomplish our objectives. Over the 12 years I have been based in a home office, I have held eight different IBM roles of increasing responsibility. Geography has never been a significant factor. Results are what matter.

IBM has adopted the notion of a *globally integrated enterprise.* The use of social business tools within the organization and in our ecosystem enables us to collaborate across geographies and time zones, across organizations and divisions. We use the right experts on the right projects without regard to time or location. This allows IBM to deploy the best resources as needed. If the right expert to work on a customer situation is thousands of miles away, it is no longer required to put that person on the next airplane to the customer location.

One challenge for us at IBM is that we are evolving quickly in this regard, and many of our clients, rightfully, still expect a human being to show up in person. I expect continued innovation in this area as virtual engagement models and tools for high-definition video meetings become more pervasive.

Measuring Return on Investment

For the social product manager at IBM, the benefits of all of these tools are clear. The omnipresence described in Chapter 7, "Tools of the Trade," is available internally. A culture of sharing (placing content and insight into forums, file sharing tools, activities, and communities) amplifies key messages and increases knowledge throughout the organization. It establishes digital reputations and makes expertise locatable. The information that used to be held closely by product managers as part of carefully controlled release cycles now empowers everyone in the organization to contribute ideas and energy toward making those products more successful.

The most frequently asked question about social business is, what is the return on investment? How can an organization measure its effectiveness in being social, and what the impact has been in terms of improved performance?

Inside IBM, we have many tools to measure our use of social business tools. For example, an automated tool called SmallBlue was created to map internal digital influence. SmallBlue takes snapshots of internal usage patterns for email, instant messaging, and social computing. By analyzing who knows what and who knows whom, SmallBlue can detect patterns of knowledge and information sharing throughout IBM.

The results of efforts like this have demonstrated that the social business tools have provided pathways for employees who previously would never interact with each other to share knowledge and leverage each other's ideas for improved results. Connections across geographic sites, organizational silos, and levels of hierarchy have all become routine at IBM, whereas in the past our information flow was more structured and compartmentalized.

One interesting and surprising metric that correlates with our adoption of social business tools is a declining rate and usage of email. My inbox used to overflow with 150 to 200 emails per day. Even as my responsibilities and staff have grown, my inbound email volume has actually been decreasing for the last couple of years, to the point where I now receive only 75 to 100 emails per day.

What has changed about the email is that it is now much more personal, instead of the old approach where so much of what I received was broadcast in nature. More of the messages sent to me now are directly actionable individual or small group communication. Email triage is now simply one set of interactions throughout a day. IBM is now building tools to deliver a social mail experience within the context of other interactions, moving away from treating email as an isolated and reactive experience.

An even more impressive statement about return on investment comes from a Rutgers/Duke University study of IBM's inside sales organization. At IBM, inside sales is often the primary face to the customer, and the sales representatives handle the entire breadth and depth of IBM's software portfolio. During late 2011 and early 2012, researchers analyzed the performance of IBM inside sales representatives, with a focus on correlating digital sales eminence—the salesperson's expertise using social tools—and network influence with sales outcomes.

The study found that

- Inside sales representatives who utilize social business tools identify 11 percent more opportunity revenue than those who do not.
- Inside sales specialists, with expertise on a particular product area, who utilize social business tools close 26 percent more opportunities than those who do not.
- Increases in a seller's digital sales eminence and network influence can increase their results by 2 percent to 6 percent.

These salespeople's results can be tied directly to the social product manager. Their increased digital eminence results from using the previously described IBM social business tools, which connect these salespeople on the front lines back to product management and other roles throughout IBM. Product managers provide information and insight both proactively and reactively to inside sales, who now can represent the solutions they have on offer more authoritatively.

One of the interesting net effects of social business tools is flattening an organization. Employees at all levels contribute, share, and learn equally. In the case of IBM's sales organization, social tools have also harmonized access to information across various roles.

The cultural change that has enabled these sellers to be more effective has placed an emphasis on responsiveness to customer requirements. "Everyone sells" has become a mantra within IBM, and product managers, engineers, and architects are all accessible as a result. The salesperson facing the customer has the entire IBM organization a click away.

IBM's widespread use of social apps, and its impact on the company's success, is demonstrative of a success in social business. Even if we had only adopted a fraction of the technology that we use today, the result would still be impressive changes in how we build and deliver products and solutions. The most important lesson has been the changing of our culture.

The Impact of Social Tools on Product Development

Success on the inside is not just about the tools in place for internal collaboration. The social product manager must also be an advocate—for customers and prospects, for market requirements, and for use of the social business tools themselves.

Social product development presents many opportunities. It is a chance to bring everyone in the process closer to the voice of the customer. It can help separate fact from anecdote. It can terminate the "telephone" game, where a message slowly morphs as it is passed along.

Just as would be done with other market research, product managers should assemble social data into meaningful, consumable information. The product manager's use of social tools inside the company helps bring the voice of the customer or prospect to the rest of their organization, as the primary agent for the marketplace. Input from social networks will help build influence, moving away from individual customer examples and toward the strength of basing discussion on the aggregate industry perspective.

For example, in 2012, my team and I were preparing for a workshop on future product direction. I asked my blog readers for input on functional areas of enhancement or new features that could be considered. Within a week, nearly 100 responses—admittedly a small subset of the market, but representative voices—had provided some clear points of potential emphasis. Though there were literally dozens of distinct ideas, some specific patterns to the initially unstructured data emerged, such that we could bring a summary representation into the meeting (see Figure 9.3).

Instead of product management providing instinctive assessment of market requirements, the blog, along with ideation sites like ideajam.net, provided a starting point for fact-based discussion. The development managers, product architects, and engineers in attendance were able to quickly assess relative priorities and potential "quick wins" for future product enhancement. If a functional area had not made the graphical representation of the blog input, it was deemed less important for future consideration.

Typically, contributors would bring anecdotal input to such a workshop. Product managers in any industry have a tendency to over-emphasize considerations raised in recent customer interactions. In this case, however, the social networking data brought the voice of the customer into the room directly—and minimized the hearsay discussion. The focus of the meeting quickly centered on specific actionable themes that were already recognized as potentially valuable in future releases. In addition to ideation or feature management system input, the crowdsourced themes provided an overarching guide for the discussion.

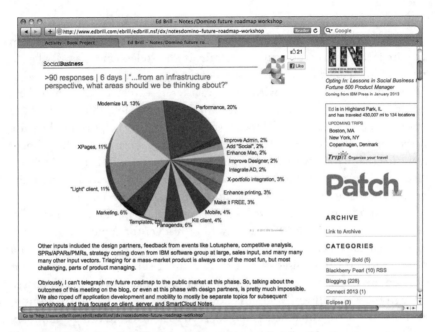

Figure 9.3   Summation of edbrill.com responses on future product direction.

Not everyone in an organization needs to "be social" for social business tools to improve the product development process. Similar to how a traditional meeting fails when everyone is talking at once, establishing lead voices for both external and internal communication will make social networking a more effective tool. In a social context, proper utilization of market input for product development or enhancement requires focus and leadership.

Occasionally, my staff are asked by customers and partners why they are not more active on external social networks. The answer is unexpected: They all participate. They just don't interact on a high-frequency basis. A product manager might author a guest blog on my website, or ask me to post content on their behalf. Otherwise, they are successful consumers of social input, not facilitators. The social tools are still important contributors to their individual and collective success, they just take a different approach to *social,* without the need to author content.

Even though these senior product managers may be less-visible externally, they are active and engaged on our internal social communities and microblogs. IBMers are, of course, part of the community of advocates for our products, and the internal feedback and discussion provides critical input and validation.

One unanticipated benefit of social networking has been reaching a broader IBM audience through what ostensibly were meant to be market-facing channels. Of my Twitter followers, blog readers, and Facebook friends, a significant subgroup includes IBM colleagues. They have chosen to interact with my social content because of the aggregation of customer voices, but this collective organizational listening also increases my influence inside the organization.

Indeed, it is entirely possible to derive all the benefits of social business as a participant or even a spectator. Social product managers can leverage and grow their authority by coaching, helping others in the organization understand what they are reading and why it is relevant. By assisting others with processing and internalizing market input, the voice of the customer reaches more deeply into an organization, often to places where it has never been heard before.

Who Needs to Participate?

During production of this book, I had the opportunity to participate in a panel discussion at Social Media Week in Chicago on the topic "The New Leadership Imperative: A Social CEO." The panel did include a chief executive who understood the value of social media, Frank Sorentino III of North Jersey Community Bank. The bank operates eight branches with assets of more than $800 million.

Sorentino described his use of Twitter, Facebook, and his blog to extend the reach of his bank. He indicated that customers who he otherwise would never interact with had become part of his networks, and as such, helped him recognize ways in which the bank could operate more effectively.

Sorentino urges others in his organization to use social media. He is one of the rare CEOs today who encourages a culture of participation. Sorentino believes that the tools of social media are no different from writing a letter or appearing on CNBC; governance still applies.

Even so, the Social Media Week panel concluded that many CEOs and C suite executives will refrain from external social media participation, because of financial disclosure regulations and other concerns about disproportionate influence. For many organizations, the best opportunity for senior executives to be part of a culture of participation is inside the organization, where they can both lead and influence simultaneously in the relative safety of internal discussion. This has definitely been a positive lesson learned at

IBM and for many of our customers. As a proof point, adoption of Connections, IBM's social business platform, is particularly widespread in regulated industries, who are primarily using it inside their organizations.

One risk of using customer perspectives to influence your organization is to lend too much weight to concepts and ideas obtained through social business tools. Chapter 10, "Risk Management in Social Business," discusses both future considerations and the risks of relying solely, or too heavily, on social conversations.

Lessons Learned

- The social product manager can lead, influence, and benefit from the cultural transformation into a social business, moving from sending to sharing.

- The social product manager can demonstrate measurable results of engagement through social tools, leading to improved sales results or more satisfied customers.

- The social product manager can carry the voice of the customer into the product development process with more authority and influence than anecdote or gut instinct.

Endnotes

[1] IBM 2012 Global CEO Study (www.ibm.com/ceostudy).

[2] Altimeter Group, Charlene Li, "Report: Making the Business Case for Enterprise Social Networks," February 22, 2012 (http://tinyurl.com/84ymm8y). Used with permission.

[3] "The New Collaboration: Enabling Innovation, Changing the Workplace." IBM white paper, January 2008.

[4] Sandy Carter, *Get Bold!: Using Social Media to Create a New Type of Social Business.* IBM Press, 2011, page 46.

[5] IDC, "Mobile Worker Population to Reach 1.3 Billion by 2015," press release, January 5, 2012 (http://tinyurl.com/86m4n9g).

IO

Risk Management in Social Business

Opting In's subtitle is "Lessons in Social Business from a Fortune 500 Product Manager." Over the past decade, my IBM colleagues and I have developed a deep understanding of the social business space, through thousands of interactions with clients, building tools, growing a business, and experiential immersion. As with every organization around the globe, there is always room for improvement. At IBM, we regularly apply our "lessons learned" in the evolution of our business, resulting in continuous adaptation and improvement.

Lest anyone walk away from this book thinking that social business is all upside, this chapter is an opportunity to examine some of the risks and concerns, at least as they exist at this moment in time.

Risk management is a core skill for product and brand managers. Your company has expended significant organizational energy to build a market and establish presence. Yet launching the product or extending product presence through the use of social tools requires a measure of caution. Inside the organization, inaccurate or early release of information can upend a product launch or sale.

The social product manager faces several new and amplified risks. In the quest to be engaged, transparent, and agile, there are several potential unintended consequences of the broadcast nature of social content, along with occasional blind spots as a result of the demographics of participation.

Even if you are already conscious of the risks of social business, or this chapter helps you take them to heart, recognize that this is often more art than science and that you will occasionally stumble. The safety net of both your personal and corporate policies and guidelines will help you recover, and your use of agility and transparency will often make the forward progress even stronger.

Risk of Reaching the Wrong Audience

In social media, there is no ability to segment your message. All social tools, whether inside your firewall or outside, are broadcast media. Although some technologies allow for selective reach, like Facebook lists, the reality is that if something is published, it can be repeated. Any attempt at *narrowing the audience* will fail.

One of the many roles I've held at IBM has been in competitive intelligence, part of our market research function. I remember the gleeful moment when I received a vendor's electronic presentation about a new product—with the speaker notes intact. One of the slides had a note that said "We do *not* want to tell customers about [a particular product limitation]." Unfortunately, this was before social media; disappointing, because I surely would have assisted them in amplifying their unintended message.

In another example, I once wrote a blog entry and tried to explicitly disclaim it as a public quote for use by journalists. Not only was my attempt ignored, I was also widely criticized for attempting to be restrictive and social at the same time. I eventually retracted the portion of the blog entry that tried to wave off reporters and apologized for even thinking that I could do so. The story moved on and the criticism stopped.

The Internet, and individual readers, have long memories. Telling one part of your audience, such as existing customers, a different message than another part, such as prospects, will eventually fail. This method may work for A | B testing, or targeted individual messages, but any broadcast must be consistent to retain credibility. Manage this risk through ensuring your outbound messages are consumable by all audiences.

The companion risk to reaching the wrong audience is the risk of *handing your competition a weapon through candor.*

A social business that does everything right—engaging with customers as individuals, conducting a dialogue rather than a monologue, being responsive to the market—still faces the risk of the right words ending up in the wrong place. The competition, industry analysts, and journalists are all reading the same words as your existing and prospective customers but with drastically different motivations.

Choosing to engage in the conversation sometimes means exposing weaknesses in your product or solution offering today. In most organizations, "we listened to your feedback and made the new product better" is in the core DNA of the product manager. Sometimes, though, acknowledging today's product deficiency could be used against you.

Decisions that seemed right at the time can also resurface, sometimes in a less-flattering present tense context. In the social realm, individuals with long memories and lasting affiliations might, even with good intentions, inadvertently bring an old failure or market misstep back into the spotlight.

In 2010, Microsoft released a new a product, and as part of the marketing materials published a competitive comparison with the corresponding IBM software solution. In the document, Microsoft argued in favor of one of their product's claimed advantages. To offer contrast with the IBM story, the Microsoft web page linked to a comment I made on one of the blog entries on edbrill.com from 2008.

The comment described how IBM had decided to cancel a new product feature that had been considered for a future release of our product. Someone at Microsoft had apparently decided to try to exploit the comment, which was clearly intended to be read by those who understood IBM's decision, and take it out of context to support their own argument.

Perhaps that example would have served as a lesson learned—not to be so publicly open about terminated product efforts. However, in this case, I felt like the risk at the time of the comment was minimal, as most of the relevant IBM customers understood our position.

Upon discovery of Microsoft's link, I chose a tactical but also somewhat risky approach to neutralizing their message. Though I rarely modify edbrill.com content after publication, the site has a disclosed policy that comments are owned by the person who posted them. In this case, as the comment was my own, I simply deleted it. Microsoft's link instead ended up sending readers to the top of the page, which happened to be a blog entry describing the advantages of the latest version of my product.

At the time of this book's publication, Microsoft still hadn't figured this out, and the deep link remains on their competitive paper today. Thank you, Microsoft, for giving me an opportunity from your website to directly talk about the benefits of an IBM solution.

Managing the "potential competitive weapon" risk takes restraint. One approach is considering every piece of content through the lens of a reader with ill intentions. How can your words be spun against you? The social product manager-as-politician is likely already adept at this skill. Another approach is to assume that the competition already knows all your weak spots, so stating them out loud is of limited additional risk. I often use the latter approach when validating feature request-type input for products; the competition likely has already thought of the same requirement, or might even already deliver it in their own product.

The Public Apology, and the Risk of Emotion

Some believe that, even as a social business, external communication must retain a positive, almost-cheerleading tone of voice. Every blog post, tweet, and LinkedIn comment should reflect the company "party line." Never admit weakness or mistakes.

I think that is an outdated point of view.

When Apple shipped the iPhone 4, there were widespread reports of telephone reception problems. The U.S. publication *Consumer Reports* conducted scientific testing and documented—on a blog—a design flaw that they indicated could be rectified with duct tape or a plastic case. They also questioned Apple's initial response to the rumors, which was to blame a supposedly erroneous display of signal strength on a software problem.[1]

Four days later, Apple's late CEO Steve Jobs held a press conference. Jobs displayed a bit of emotion and expressed frustration that the situation had been "blown so out of proportion that it is incredible."[2] However, to address the telephone signal problem, Apple offered every iPhone 4 customer either a free plastic case to help with reception or a refund on their purchase. The antenna issue actually evaporated in the market once it was acknowledged and a solution was offered.

What would have happened to iPhone sales if Jobs had not eventually accepted responsibility for a problem and committed to resolve it? No one knows, though it seems likely that a denial would have dented sales and

Apple's reputation. In the feeding frenzy over the signal strength and reception issue, bloggers and other social media voices were catalysts that eventually forced Apple to respond. In answering the social media pressure, Apple turned crisis into opportunity. They went on to sell 70 million iPhone 4 units worldwide—continuing their success after only a small speed bump.

The public apology has an important place in building digital reputation and influence. In a social business, it is important to be seen as fallible, human, and transparent. Going beyond honesty as the best policy, the idea that the humans running a business can acknowledge when they have or had the opportunity to do better is a clear signal to the market of openness and responsiveness. If a customer knows that they can count on their vendor to make a situation right if it ever goes wrong, and will do so in an open and forthright way, the customer will likely place significant value on the trust that is formed as a by-product of candor.

However, one of the risks in social business is the *human element of emotion.* In the heat of picking a fight, or playing defense, humans will sometimes overreact or choose the wrong words. It is hard to retract social media, as Google quickly caches content or tweets are saved for posterity. It is critically important to think through the way readers will react to your writing, every time you engage.

In social media, it is easy to bring others into a conversation, perhaps overreaching in terms of the necessary audience or amplification of a particular topic. When the participants in a discussion are people who know each other, and therefore use more casual language or private references, the tone of human interaction can be misinterpreted.

A common technique to attempt to attract attention through social media, or for that matter through email, is to add someone in a relatively senior position to an interaction. This practice is sometimes described as name checking or name dropping. The belief is that the name drop will create urgency or compel action for the other recipients by drawing them into a conversation, typically a negatively charged one.

Name checking is one of the risks of establishing a social presence. A disgruntled customer, especially a "digital native" who is used to using online communication as a primary vehicle, will find it natural to directly attack you or your brand/product through social networks.

As a social product manager, if you are name-checked, a situation analysis is quickly needed to determine whether it merits your attention. Unfortunately, such a situation offers little upside. Responding validates the decision and action of the name checker. Asking questions of the other recipients may inadvertently amplify the original situation, perhaps unnecessarily. Ignoring the whole thing might alienate a key customer or prospect in a situation that could actually have been important or relevant.

With social networks bringing personal conversations out into public view, the emotional risk of participation takes on an additional dimension, that of becoming too close to the customer or market. While sometimes it is a natural human instinct to sympathize with customer complaints or criticisms, the social product manager has only so much influence. Taking on every problem runs the risk of turning purely reactive, or feeling pressured to try to resolve issues and diffuse situations. That could lead to mistakes or overreaching beyond areas where the product manager has influence.

As another example, in one of my attempts to diffuse criticism, I inadvertently launched a personal attack on someone who wasn't even involved in the conversation.

A consultant had written a blog entry that expressed a lack of confidence in where a particular product was going. He went so far in this blog entry as to question whether he should continue his affiliation with IBM as a vendor. However, rather than make such a decision, he simply posed the question rhetorically. In a comment on his blog, I drew an unflattering comparison to another consultant whom we both knew; we'll call him Max. Though the example was similar and possibly even relevant, Max was not involved in this conversation in any way.

Unsurprisingly, Max was alerted to my comparison and was offended at being used as an example. Max then proceeded to send senior IBM executives public tweets with links to the discussion, questioning why he was being criticized. Awareness of the tension accelerated online.

This *ad hominem* attack was the only time I ran afoul of IBM's Social Computing Guidelines, and it was a genuine, human mistake. I was too close to the people involved, and instead of staying on the topic of the product or marketplace, I crossed a line and got personal. The only way to diffuse the original attempt at diffusion was a public apology, which was both the right thing to do and the right emotion to feel at the time.

Max accepted my apology, as did the others who participated in the conversation. The senior IBM executives reminded me of our policies, and the situation diffused. The next time I saw Max, we rebuilt some bridges. In the end, we both shared the same passionate goal of succeeding in the market, and we learned something more about how we could do so together. That seemed like a valuable lesson learned.

The Risk of Subset Population through Language and Other Demographics

Today, English is spoken by at least half a billion people on the planet. However, it is not the most popular native language; Mandarin Chinese holds that title. Spanish, Arabic, and Russian are also spoken by hundreds of millions of people.

An English-language blog or discussion forum will mainly attract those comfortable discussing the subject matter in English. In China, the social network Tencent QQ has more than 700 million active user accounts. Orkut, one of the first social networks, is long-forgotten in most of the world, except in Brazil, where the Google-owned service is still used by 66 million users.

As such, social business carries the significant risk of *engaging only a subset population.*

On edbrill.com, 30 percent of the visits come from the United States; another 20 percent come from English-speaking countries, including the United Kingdom, Canada, and Australia. Therefore, it seems likely that the majority of readers speak English natively. The converse statistics prove the point better: Only 1 percent of visits come from Japan, another 1 percent from China, and another 1 percent from Brazil. Despite the huge online populations in those countries, very few land on my website.

There are other subset population factors online. For example, those participating in social media may fall into only certain age groups, rather than the entire spectrum of current or potential buyers for a product. In a business-to-business scenario, the dialogue may include only influencers rather than decision makers, or only specialists in one particular discipline rather than the entire line of business. The real intended audience might not even know that a community or blog or Facebook page exists or that there is any opportunity to interact between vendor and customer.

Therefore, turning to a blog or other social network for market research requires a filter. On my blog, for example, comments only originate from a small percentage of readers to begin with; those from non-native English speakers are an even smaller fraction. Additional tools besides the blog, such as Twitter and online forums, or more traditional market research methods, are needed to validate industry trends in those countries.

Another approach is a cloning exercise. Is there someone else—preferably inside your organization, but even a trusted partner or distributor—who can represent your interests online in other languages? Perhaps the desire to have global reach provides a mentoring opportunity for staff in regional offices or some other link in your distribution or supply. That representative can translate content, or even initiate their own unique voice, based on the social product manager's guidance.

Dachis Group analyst Olga Kozanecka identified the linguistics gap in an April 2012 blog post. Speaking of research on European social brand experiences, Kozanecka wrote, "Europe is a challenging market in terms of geographic, linguistic and cultural fragmentation; levels of personal adoption of social media differ across countries, and sometimes there are local variants of social networks as well as the major platforms like Facebook. As a consequence, brands need a more sophisticated social strategy that makes social presence local and relevant yet scalable across countries and channels."[3]

Kozanecka identifies a blended approach, mixing centralized and uniform content strategy with local and fragmented execution. As part of an interview conducted during production of this book, she further identified Unilever as an organization successfully addressing the linguistics, geographic, and cultural considerations of their social media strategy.

As discussed during Social Media Week 2012, Unilever uses a single URL for its Facebook channel, but renders a country-specific page based on Internet address. The content provided is a mixture of global information authored centrally within the organization, and local content, in local language, produced locally. Unilever uses predefined templates for their Facebook channel to guarantee consistency across markets. Unilever believes this global approach to Facebook successfully addresses the challenges of linguistics and geography.

Risk of Identity Challenges and Imitations

In an online world of digital reputation, potential infringements on trademarks, branding, or individual identity pose risks of *confusion or misappropriation of presence.* There are still relatively few tools to protect individual brands or reputations on public social networks. Although Twitter offers a "verified identity" mark, there is no way to ask for this service; it is solely at Twitter's discretion. Otherwise, individual and brand/company names are, unfortunately, easily imitated on most networks. Usually, some kind of appeal process to challenge the authenticity of an account exists, but this takes time and effort.

The social product manager can use all of the same tools of situation analysis and amplification when confronting infringement online. Where it is of a critical nature, engaging or picking a fight may be worthwhile. Often, though, it is best ignored. In many cases, fans and fanatics adopt brand identity, sharing and amplifying appreciation for a product or service. The tools remain the same: choose to engage or ignore. Often this decision will mirror the strategy in place for your brand's overall Internet presence and identity. If you believe in protecting your brand at all costs, even the fan pages will present issues. However, I encourage you to try where possible to allow these independent voices to persist. These human elements help expand awareness and can even, at times, enhance digital reputation.

"Fake" Twitter accounts number in the thousands, and some are even verified accounts! A few years ago, a @FakeEdBrill appeared, somehow tweeting about the same conferences and events I was attending, along with some of the same topics. @FakeEdBrill is not malicious in intent and is actually very funny. However, many of the parody accounts on Twitter are cynical at a minimum, and some are angry or critical.

Another identity risk is spam. The ill-intentioned of the world have also discovered the public social networks and attempt to insert their messages on blog comments, Twitter replies and hashtags, Facebook page comments, and Instagram @ mentions. All of these can affect your individual or corporate brand and digital reputation.

I am fortunate to have selected a blogging engine, based on my own products, that is highly resistant to comment spam. Still, every day, I check through recently received comments on edbrill.com to purge out the ones that get through. In a good versus evil mindset, I also take the time to flag spammers on Twitter and block their accounts from reaching me. This is all a time investment, and one where it may be useful to recruit some advocates to assist.

Nothing extinguishes my interest in reading a blogger's writing more than a site full of comment spam. It signals to the reader that the site owner is not interested in his or her responsibility as curator. Be sure to protect your digital reputation and make the time to clean up. Hopefully the tools will evolve and spam will be less of a problem in the future.

Parody, criticism, fans, and advocates are all elements of social networking. As such, brand and identity infringement is simply another element of life online where risk exists. The best tool to manage this risk and influence the conversation, though, remains your own unique voice.

Internal Risks

Social networking inside an organization can sometimes risk *unintended or premature disclosure of information.*

With good intentions and much upside, a cultural change from sending to sharing results in a lot more of a company's decision-making process taking place out in the open. More stakeholders are involved, more perspectives are considered. I am a strong advocate for the use of internal versions of social business tools; there is tremendous value to deploying private, inside-the-company tools to foster innovation and flatten the organization.

However, many internal discussions require confidentiality or restricted participation. Social business doesn't change basic operational characteristics.

Where this risk becomes real is at the edges. While discussion of a potential acquisition or merger is clearly something that is a need-to-know topic in most organizations, an innocent question posted in an internal forum might inadvertently share secondhand information or spark the rumor mill related to the effort. A secret new product introduction, where timing is critical, can be foiled by an administrative assistant trying to find out why so many people in a shared community are traveling to the same place on the same date. Humans are naturally inquisitive, and social tools help feed that instinct.

During the writing of this book, my team and I made an important decision to change a forthcoming product's branding and version number. The decision was made with surprising agility, in response to many internal and external feedback vectors. As a social business, we were rapidly practicing what we preach.

However, once the decision was made, we recognized it would take a few months to fully implement. A project team assembled and, as a typical first step, assembled a presentation on the objectives of the new product branding, along with the transition steps and risks along the way.

Because of the significant market impact of brand transition, the team was told to keep their communications within the team and their management only. However, as a social business, one team member—almost by rote—posted the draft presentation in a shared repository. Instantly, rumors abounded about the upcoming product transition.

An argument could be made that even this unintentional premature disclosure to a broad audience had upside potential. The community now exposed to the planned change could provide their own input and support for the project. More points of view could equal more potential routes for success.

However, the presentation alone could not communicate the full perspective and story of how the decision to change had been made nor the complete message for the market on the day of announcement. Incomplete information spread widely risks having others take action without the full picture of a plan or coordination with others who are part of the effort.

In short, confidentiality and private communication are still important tools in organizational communication. They can be made more effective within workgroups and teams through the use of social business policy. The overall risk to inadvertent internal communication can then be managed through a mix of private and broadcast tools within the organization.

Lessons Learned

- The social product manager must manage elements of risk that exist despite the broad and deep reach of social business tools.

- Reaching the wrong audience, getting emotional, and language are all risks that should factor into the social product manager's communications strategy.

- The risks of social business exist internally as well, typically around premature disclosure or moving private communication into open channels.

Endnotes

[1] Consumer Reports, Lab tests: Why Consumer Reports can't recommend the iPhone 4, July 12, 2010.

[2] New York Times: Updates from Apple's Discussion of iPhone 4 Problem, July 16, 2010.

[3] Dachis Group, Olga Kozanecka, "Why are brands in Europe falling short of expectations?" April 16, 2012. Used with permission.

11

Putting *Opting In* into Practice

After ten chapters, the promise and opportunities of social business are pulsing through your veins. You understand the affinity that product and brand managers have for all things social, both in the marketplace at large and within your organization. You are ready to jump into social sites, start playing offense, and activate your advocates.

Only one question remains: What now?

This final chapter addresses how to apply the concepts explored throughout *Opting In* as part of the daily performance of your work, in three sections:

1. A fictional brand manager named Samantha shows what the typical day in the life of a social product manager offers.
2. How to use the "lessons learned" from throughout *Opting In.*
3. A glimpse into the future of the social product manager

A Day in the Life

My business school experience emphasized the importance of case studies and role playing. To help take the lessons of *Opting In* outside of the technology industry, the following is a fictional case study. The example discusses opportunities for social engagement as part of the launch of a new service in the highly competitive airline industry.

Samantha Daryn is a brand manager for Startup Airlines. Startup formed in 2010, with a small fleet of late-model airplanes operating North American flights out of a few strategic airports across the United States.

Samantha's responsibility is to increase participation in Startup's customer rewards program, Startup Options. Frequent fliers and other affinity customers earn "shares" in Startup Options by flying, through other travel transactions, and by using an affiliated co-branded credit card. Her goals for the next six months include growing Startup Airlines' business travel customer base.

Samantha knows that the airline industry is extremely competitive and relatively commoditized. Fliers generally care about schedule, cost, and perks, in different priority depending on whether they personally pay the bill. Startup Airlines is too small to compete on schedule, but they are price competitive and differentiating on perks when possible.

Samantha and her team recognize that perks cost money, but they are the only real vehicle for creating affinity and loyalty to the airline. She works closely with her marketing organization to ensure that even the smallest perks—such as complimentary newspapers in the waiting lounge—are highlighted in Startup Airlines' outbound messages.

Startup Airlines has made a strategic decision to offer in-flight Internet Wi-Fi access at no charge. The belief is that the free service will help Startup Airlines attract more business customers. The competition is currently charging between $8 and $15 per flight for Internet access, most of which goes to the provider rather than to the airline. Startup quietly negotiated a fixed-price contract with the Internet service provider for a one-year period. By the time the contract has to be renegotiated, the price of such services should decrease, or other airlines will have matched Startup Airlines and they will be forced to continue to offer the no-charge service.

Samantha has been concerned whether Startup Airlines can launch an effective marketing campaign to capitalize on the free service. Through *internal discussion forums,* Startup's brand management and marketing teams have been sharing ideas for how to create awareness of the new in-flight perk, in a way that will capture attention from the business travelers they are targeting.

Startup Airlines is still too small to have frequency tier levels in the Startup Options loyalty program. Other airlines use these elite status tiers to identify and reward their most loyal, elite customers. However, Samantha has been slowly building up a database of Startup Airlines "angels," key customers who have been vocal supporters on public social networks, using *alerts* and *monitoring tools.*

Today, Samantha is excited because she is about to reach out to the angels for the first time. Startup Airlines has decided to activate the new free Wi-Fi service. Samantha has found that 50 of her angels happen to be flying today. She starts the day working with Startup's community manager to *access the company Twitter ID* and send these angels direct messages or public tweets alerting them to the in-flight perk. She suggests a *hashtag* of #StartupFreeWiFi.

Onboard, the welcome page of the new Wi-Fi facility also carries the #StartupFreeWiFi hashtag, and a *button to tweet about the new service.* Samantha has one computer in her office monitoring that hashtag stream, and sure enough, within minutes the angels are singing:

> "@SocialBrilliance: Wow, Startup Airlines has free in-flight wifi today! #StartupFreeWifi"

> "@AKASwissCheese: This tweet from 20,000 feet, courtesy of #StartupFreeWiFi"

> "@MilesPerLitre: Didn't know they cared! Startup Airlines offering everyone free wifi now! #StartupFreeWiFi"

Samantha signals her communications counterparts to unleash their press release, and for her marketing colleagues to update the company website with the new perk.

Quickly, Samantha discovers a new topic has been started on the flyertalk.com frequent flyer chat board, discussing Startup Airlines' new offer. Suddenly, hundreds of people are talking about the airline and in-flight Wi-Fi, with everyone putting a personal spin on the story. By noon, CNBC is featuring the news, along with quotes from the #StartupFreeWiFi Twitter stream.

After a few crazy hours, Samantha checks back in with Startup's community manager. @StartupAirlines has been *flooded with tweets,* including several messages from the angels. They have been requesting details, and the *FAQ* (Frequently Asked Questions) that Samantha prepared is getting hundreds of hits on the airline's website.

Samantha has activated her advocates while going strongly on offense. With little proactive outreach, Startup has successfully leveraged social business tools. Better yet, Samantha has recruited her army, who are now in tune with the airline and its social network presence. To encourage loyalty, which after all is Samantha's main goal, she adds one share to the Startup Options account of each #StartupFreeWiFi tweeter. The positive *feedback loop* will ensure that the angels help advocate for the airline, that day and into the future.

Using the "Lessons Learned"

Opting In contains 35 "Lessons Learned" in the preceding chapters. Some are individual coaching points, whereas others envision your role as an organizational change agent. In putting *Opting In* into practice, each of these lessons has been aggregated and placed into one of these four broad categories:

1. How will your product/service and organization benefit from becoming a social business?
2. Why should you be a social product manager?
3. What are the opportunities for a social product manager?
4. How does the role of a product/brand manager change as part of a social business transformation?

The sections that follow examine the lessons learned in the context of these four questions.

Benefits of a Social Business

Social business is a transformational vision of how an organization operates, along with its relationships with customers, suppliers, partners, and the marketplace. Organizations must opt in to social business as a key component of innovation, best practice, and understanding the market.

Social business provides new tools that will result in improved performance, communication, and responsiveness, but both technology adoption and cultural change are required to successfully take advantage of those tools. The result is an organization that is more engaged in the market, transparent in its actions, and agile in its decision making.

A social business encompasses a broader spectrum of voices than its own employees. A marketplace of advocates carries and amplifies messages about your product/service to current and prospective customers, adding its own digital reputation and endorsement to the brand perception and value of your offering.

Social business has risks that must be managed, though in many ways those are no different from other forms of communication. The broad and deep reach of social networking increases the volume on your organization's messages, but usually will still reach only a subset of the market. Conversely, messages may be amplified beyond the original audience and taken out of context. Linguistics, geography, and cultural norms of participation will affect the success of social business tools in contributing to your product/service's success. The risks of social business also exist internally and must be factored into your organization's policies and guidelines around the use of social computing tools.

Becoming a Social Product Manager

The opportunities for combining social business and product/brand management are clear. Social product managers, through better access to both customers/prospects and information, increase their marketplace understanding and ability to identify product/service requirements and improve their decision making.

Social product managers define themselves in the context of their personal brand—establishing leadership, expertise, authenticity, and credibility, while demonstrating willingness to take risks. Social product managers represent themselves, their product, and their company, all to a greater degree than previously possible, due to the reach and amplification of their unique voice.

Social product managers influence market perception of their product/ service. Their mere presence indicates passion, confidence, and belief in their product. Social product managers can help transform their organization's culture, embedding social into business process and moving from merely sending information to sharing. The social product manager carries the voice of the customer into the product development process, with more authority and influence than anecdote or gut instinct.

In addition to all the clear and tangible benefits of becoming a social product manager, your transformation will lead to an improved ability to connect people with information and people with people. In the process, you will make more friends and have more fun at being a product/brand manager.

Opportunities for Social Product Managers

The social product manager can create new opportunities simply by having conversations about ideas. The social product manager offers a unique voice and perspective to the marketplace, one that originates information and ideas and responds authoritatively.

The social product manager can act as a trusted human guide or curator of content for customers and potential buyers. They can deliver the right experiences through social tools for prospects to move through the sales process and turn into satisfied customers.

On both an outbound and inbound basis, the social product manager can leverage the digital grapevine to obtain feedback directly from customers, prospective buyers, and competitors. They can demonstrate measurable results of engagement through social tools, leading to improved sales results or more satisfied customers.

The Changing Role of the Product/Brand Manager

The social product manager must account for three dimensions of individual success: self, product, and company. They must communicate transparently and honestly and act with agility. These behaviors earn credibility and support more strongly than spin or market-speak.

Social product managers are most effective when they properly analyze situations, instead of simply reacting. Messages are different on offense versus defense, and must have the appropriate volume and action/reaction as part of their force. Timing is a critical variable in social business. Sometimes, no communication remains better than engaging.

Social product managers must develop their anticipatory insight. They must consider potential unintended consequences of communication given the human nature and broad reach of social tools. Sometimes, it is appropriate for the social product manager to create or engage in conflict, but only with properly set expectations of the results.

Even as social product managers use tools to amplify their messages and reach, real-world interactions can further amplify messages and activate advocates. The social product manager can leverage real-world activities and endorsements to influence communities and build individual relationships.

These lessons learned form the foundation of success for a product/brand manager. Though the concepts will remain the same, the tools and behaviors will change in the future. Success for the social product manager results from having the raw skills to adapt to a rapidly changing environment and culture and an understanding of how to use the tools as they evolve.

The Social Product Manager of the Future

The influence of social business is only just beginning in most organizations. Awareness of the need for and opportunity from the transformation to social is increasing, but like the adoption of the Internet itself, evolution will accelerate and drive even more recognition of value.

The social product manager can expect additional transformation along four dimensions: organizational alignment, inclusiveness, selectivity, and technology. Each of these is worth additional exploration.

Organizational Alignment

At IBM, over past two years we have worked with hundreds of chief marketing officers and chief information officers on the need for their two missions to be carefully aligned. Marketing is now one of the primary consumers and drivers of information technology in organizations today, both outbound through e-commerce and inbound through analytics. Successful organizations are coordinating activities and plans between these two functions to move from reactive to proactive, often bringing the CIO to the strategic decision-making table from the outset.

Product management as a discipline also needs some organizational realignment. In many organizations, product management is seen as an extension function—from research and development, from marketing, or even from finance. In other companies, product management sits in the center of the ecosystem, influencing all the other functional departments and roles.

The social product manager's place is not only in the hub of go-to-market activity within the organization but at the nexus of the entire marketplace. By decreasing the distance between the brand manager and the individual customer—or flat-out disintermediating parts of the value chain—the social product manager commands knowledge and influences direction, both inside and outside the company.

Recognizing the increasing number of orbital rings, both inside the organization and in the wider marketplace, more organizations will align their organizational structure around the product management function. Influence as currency will become stronger. Results will be the only key metric, instead of tasks completed. The social product manager will be able to demonstrate those results because of the direct connection to market input and feedback.

Inclusiveness

Chapter 10, "Risk Management in Social Business," discussed one of the risks of social business: blind spots due to linguistics or cultural participation barriers. It is my hope that the evolution of the social product manager provides ways to eliminate these obstacles.

Already, public social networks are evolving quickly to address both geography and language. Facebook has added in-line links to foreign-language wall postings, offering one-click machine translation. In the past, when my global friends posted in Russian or Japanese, cutting and pasting their text into Google Translate or other such services was ineffective and lost the train of thought. Now, instead of hiding or ignoring them, I can see what they have to say within the context of using Facebook.

Twitter's "trending topics" also is a major step toward inclusiveness. Twitter often feels like a large party-like gathering; there are many simultaneous conversations, but the only ones you are involved in, or even listening to, are the ones from people you know or are introduced to. Visiting a trending topic is like moving to another part of the room, without your friends; you might know what the conversation is about, but you don't know who the people discussing it are. Trending topics provide a window into other interesting threads, without having to be brought into them. This is especially important in cultures that avoid participation; digital natives are overcoming historical inhibitors and getting involved in public interaction.

Curation will help with the evolution toward greater inclusiveness. Social product managers, salespersons, or marketers can provide a human face to their organization. Buyers and prospects are more likely to engage if they can connect with someone whose reputation is established. "Click here to chat with a customer service agent" functionality will fade, except as a call center type of operation. Instead, "click here to connect with our foremost expert on the topic, whose resumé is right here so you can trust them" will compel information seekers to connect.

Selectivity

Another risk identified in Chapter 10 was the broadcast nature of social business tools. As much as inclusiveness is likely to increase in the future, so is the need to be more judicious about audience.

My first job after college graduation was with Florists' Transworld Delivery Association, or FTD as they are better known. FTD's Floral Network division is responsible for the technology infrastructure that enables customers to purchase flowers for local delivery to anywhere in the United States.

In addition to transmitting orders, the Floral Network was used to communicate messages from the Association out to member florists. One of the tools we used for marketing purposes was a *slimcast,* which sent messages to a subset of florists based on their size or geography.

Today, analytics engines already demonstrate the ability to deliver selective offers to key customers or prospects. In the future, the social product manager will leverage similar tools to slimcast, interacting with specific groups of existing customers or prospects for real-time input and feedback.

The most important place for selectivity will be internal use of social business tools. Identifying and bringing together project teams will become an exercise in identifying subject matter expertise and talent, not looking at organizational charts for the right role or title. The composition of those project teams will be more fluid in nature, with members entering and exiting as part of specific tasks or milestones rather than start to finish.

Selectivity will also be relevant in advocacy. Providing offers and opportunities to all 50,000 people who like the Facebook page for a particular retail store is old-school media insertion. Instead, the social product manager will be able to identify those most likely to respond to a particular offer, increasing response rates and building loyalty in the process.

Technology

Today, social business tools are more outbound than inbound. There are myriad ways to share content, leading end users to overshare rather than focus. The technology platform for social business will evolve in ways that make the content itself less relevant and instead align focus to results.

In 2011, IBM unveiled Watson, the first supercomputer designed to answer natural-language questions. Watson competed in the first and only computer versus human game show in history, beating Jeopardy's previous reigning champions handily.

Rather than having humans initiate searches, Watson was able to parse natural language queries into answers, in real time. Today, Watson technologies are the basis for systems implemented in banks, hospitals, and governments, solving complex problems.

Watson demonstrated the power of technology as a decision engine. The social product manager of the future will be able to use decision support technology and analytics to assess market sentiment, determine consumer preferences, and evaluate competition without the intermediate requirement of research.

As an additional component of the social business, decision engines will ensure that the voice of the customer is drawn even closer into the product development lifecycle. Bad ideas will be extinguished before ever surfacing as a prototype. Good ideas will be accelerated based on higher confidence in market success. Innovation will be an even more important differentiator, as being first to market in new categories commands an even higher premium.

Next Steps

Now that you are ready to adopt the ideas and lessons from *Opting In,* what should you do next?

Ensure That Your Organization Has a Social Computing Policy

IBM's adoption of guidelines for blogging and other online interaction in 2005 marked a fundamental change in the corporate culture. For the first time, we wrote a policy collectively, taking input from all corners of the company. The guidelines were specifically written to empower employees to be part of a culture of participation. They promised to support employees who engaged in dialogue, and encouraged others to consume and curate. In turn, the publication of these guidelines (also included here as Appendix A, "IBM Social Computing Guidelines") catalyzed the internal creation and adoption of social business tools, which are now part and parcel of the fabric of the company.

Whereas a policy and tools alone will not turn your company into a social business, they are the fundamental ingredients. Employees must know what is acceptable and what is out of bounds in terms of external communication. Some organizations are more successful at enacting such a policy when it comes with ambassadors, coaches, or training.

Social networking policy creation and adoption must be driven by a leader: human resources, corporate communications, or a CIO, with endorsement from finance, legal, and senior executives. Sometimes, marketing organizations are the catalyst, as a way to define their own role in external communication versus desired participation. Regardless of who owns the creation, ensure that all functional and geographic constituents within your organization have the opportunity to provide input. Once adopted, ensure that the policies are communicated broadly, including during the process of bringing new hires into the organization.

It is also important to ensure that executives and leaders throughout the organization are invested in not only the empowerment aspect of such a policy but also the protection component. Employees must feel confident that, should a challenge to their proper use of social business tools ever arise, the company will stand behind them.

Survey Tools Available to You, and Adopt New Ones as Appropriate

Anyone can use Twitter or Facebook for outbound social networking, and there are myriad blog delivery services, such as WordPress. The costs and entry barriers to get started on the social business journey are minimal. Inside your organization, you may consider "fit for business" tools such as IBM Connections, which is available for software deployment or in IBM's SmartCloud pay-as-you-go service. The cloud approach offers the additional benefit of being able to seamlessly integrate collaboration from customers, partners, and suppliers, all on a single platform.

The basic building blocks for social business are blogs/microblogs, wikis, social file sharing, communities, profiles/networks, tagging, social bookmarking, along with email, e-meeting, and instant messaging components. As discussed in Chapter 7, "Tools of the Trade," selection and use of these tools depends very much on your requirements and inbound/outbound strategy.

You should work with your organization's marketing and community experts to identify your owned properties, and determine what elements of social can be injected into them. On ibm.com, we added experts to a variety of product pages, giving customers a chance to connect to a human guide. My widget invites ibm.com visitors to connect with me on LinkedIn, my Facebook persona page, or Twitter. It takes readers away from our website, but keeps them connected to IBM overall.

One challenge is the constant introduction of new social networking environments. According to AddThis.com, at the time of writing there are more 330 public sharing environments. It is hard to predict which ones will succeed and which will fail. Today I use several services in addition to those described in this book: Pintrest, Google+, Digg, Posterous, Path, Tumblr, and Instagram. Too much investment in new channels risks wasting time for minimal incremental value. Go where your customers and prospects are. Leave the rest alone.

Identify Your Advocates and Determine a Mechanism to Recognize and Reward Them

No matter how large or small your industry or market, it is too big for you to carry your message alone. Geography, time, language, and audience are all variables that can interfere with successful communication and collaboration. Whether you can name them one by one, or need industrial-strength analytics tools to identify them, find those advocates who are passionate about what you make and enlist them to carry your voice.

Some advocates will avoid any connection to the vendor of their favorite product. They will want to appear neutral and unbiased. That's fine. Advocacy is not an expectation of a commitment. In identifying and rewarding advocates, be careful in choosing champions who will work with you, not against you. It is acceptable, and perhaps even encouraged, for them to be balanced in their enthusiasm. Yet lending your support, your brand, and your personal capital to build their credibility along with yours should come with some comfort they will not openly criticize or undercut your messages. Provide alternate channels for negative feedback, so it need not be aired publicly. Make yourself available—anytime, anywhere.

Recognition is easy to offer to your advocates. As Joyce Davis said about the IBM Champions program in Chapter 6, "Activate Your Advocates," don't underestimate the value of some branded merchandise. Yet rewards need not cost money. Invitations to activities and events, early disclosure or communication, or samples and previews of your product are all steps you would normally take in the course of product introduction and market research. The benefit of an active community of proponents is that they are empowered to simply tell you what you are doing right and wrong, without friction.

Recognize that advocates will come and go over time. Occasionally, I survey my LinkedIn network and wonder about contacts where I have lost touch. After two decades in this industry, it is no surprise that others have moved on to new opportunities, technologies, or industries. At the same time, there are new names and networking requests every week. There is no need to offer eternal recognition, just work together with your supporters of the moment and help make each other more successful.

Find Your Comfort Level

Not everyone needs to speak to be social. Active listening is an artful talent. Responsive commentary is a fine way to get started. Though product managers often act as coordination hubs, being the center of social activity is unnecessary. Participate in a way and at a level that makes sense for you.

When you establish a comfort level engaging with your marketplace, create and develop your unique voice. Remember that product managers are often the source of information; others in your organization simplify or amplify those messages. You should be selective about where and when you offer that voice, as it provides validation and influence.

Value quality over quantity. Twitter and blogs often create an automatic anxiety over "old" content. The date of last posting feels like the expiration date on a milk carton, there for everyone to see.

At the same time, don't let this pressure get to you. Speak when you have something to say. Readership builds gradually. If you use your unique voice, you will build an audience. Remember to be interactive—respond to tweets, comments, and blog posts. The more you build your individual brand, the more the marketplace will engage with you.

Ask for feedback. Customers and prospects are all too willing to tell you what you are doing right and wrong. Sometimes they just need to be prompted, to know that it is safe for them to share their perspective. Open up and let them in. Be transparent. Admit when you make mistakes. Build trust in the same way you do with colleagues or even friends and family.

Take an occasional break. Twitter will still be there in the morning. It is all right if someone is wrong on the Internet. Someone else is reading, too, and more likely than not, the army of advocates you've developed will help with correction and perception.

Conclusion

I hope you have enjoyed reading *Opting In* as much as I enjoyed writing it. Please feel free to share your feedback. My Twitter ID is @edbrill, my Facebook page is Facebook.com/edbrilldotcom, my blog is at edbrill.com, and my email address is ed_brill@us.ibm.com.

Of course, you can also leave feedback for this book on amazon.com or other such sites. That would be the social way, after all.

IBM Social Computing Guidelines

In the spring of 2005, I participated in an IBM internal group effort—using a wiki and other social tools, of course—to create a set of guidelines for all IBMers who wanted to blog. These guidelines aimed to provide helpful, practical advice to protect both IBM bloggers and IBM. Over seven years, the guidelines have only been updated twice—in 2008 and again in 2010—to keep pace with evolving technologies and online social tools and to ensure that they remain current to the needs of employees and the company. These efforts have broadened the scope of the existing guidelines to include all forms of social computing, while ensuring they remain current to the needs of employees and IBM.

The guidelines were created in what still feels to me as a true testimonial to the cultural transformation of a social business. The initial effort was spearheaded by David Berger, whose role in IBM's corporate communications organization would today likely be described as a "social media manager." Berger was a true pioneer in an organization that was at the time entirely used to working with planned, coordinated messages and designated spokespeople. Social media expanded and changed their mission, and he recognized the need to embrace the change.

Berger and another corporate communications manager, Christopher Barger, enlisted participation in the effort from IBMers who were already using blogging and other early social tools. Notably absent from the working group: human resources, finance, and legal. Although all of those functional areas eventually had to approve the guidelines, the participation from many different lines of business and different roles throughout the global company provided a ready group of advocates for the effort, and resulted in rapid adoption.

Many observers are surprised by a key aspect of the guidelines: They inform employees what desired behavior looks like, rather than what the employees cannot do. Most company policy documents are a long list of prohibitions, whereas the Social Computing Guidelines are an encouragement.

As a result, the majority of IBMers participate in internal and external social networks globally, confident that their employer endorses and supports their activity.

Following are the current (as of October 2012) and official IBM Social Computing Guidelines.

Introduction: Responsible Engagement in Innovation and Dialogue

Online collaboration platforms are fundamentally changing the way IBMers work and engage with each other, clients, and partners.

IBM is increasingly exploring how online discourse through social computing can empower IBMers as global professionals, innovators, and citizens. These individual interactions represent a new model: not mass communications, but masses of communicators. Through these interactions, IBM's greatest asset—the expertise of its employees—can be shared with clients, shareholders, and the communities in which it operates.

Therefore, it is very much in IBM's interest—and, we believe, in each IBMer's own—to be aware of and participate in this sphere of information, interaction and idea exchange:

To learn: As an innovation-based company, we believe in the importance of open exchange—between IBM and its clients, and among the many constituents of the emerging business and societal ecosystem—for learning. Social computing is an important arena for organizational and individual development.

To contribute: IBM—as a business, as an innovator and as a corporate citizen—makes important contributions to the world, to the future of business and technology, and to public dialogue on a broad range of societal issues. Because our business activities provide transformational insight and high-value innovation for business, government, education, healthcare, and nongovernmental organizations, it is important for IBM and IBMers to share with the world the exciting things we're learning and doing.

In 1997, IBM actively recommended that its employees use the Internet—at a time when many companies were seeking to restrict their employees' Internet access. In 2003, the company made a strategic decision to embrace the blogosphere and to encourage IBMers to participate. We continue to advocate IBMers' responsible involvement today in this rapidly growing environment of relationship, learning, and collaboration.

IBM Social Computing Guidelines

Know and follow IBM's Business Conduct Guidelines. [The Business Conduct Guidelines are a separate policy document, published annually, and also available publicly on ibm.com. The BCGs cover employee conduct in a variety of typical situations and decision-making activities at every level of the organization.]

IBMers are personally responsible for the content they publish on-line, whether in a blog, social computing site, or any other form of user-generated media. Be mindful that what you publish will be public for a long time—protect your privacy and take care to understand a site's terms of service.

Identify yourself—name and, when relevant, role at IBM—when you discuss IBM or IBM-related matters, such as IBM products or services. You must make it clear that you are speaking for yourself and not on behalf of IBM.

If you publish content online relevant to IBM in your personal capacity use a disclaimer such as this: *"The postings on this site are my own and don't necessarily represent IBM's positions, strategies, or opinions."*

Respect copyright, fair use, and financial disclosure laws.

Don't provide IBM's or another's confidential or other proprietary information and never discuss IBM business performance or other sensitive matters publicly.

Don't cite or reference clients, partners, or suppliers without their approval. When you do make a reference, link back to the source. Don't publish anything that might allow inferences to be drawn which could embarrass or damage a client.

Respect your audience. Don't use ethnic slurs, personal insults, obscenity, or engage in any conduct that would not be acceptable in IBM's workplace. You should also show proper consideration for others' privacy and for topics that may be considered objectionable or inflammatory—such as politics and religion.

Be aware of your association with IBM in online social networks. If you identify yourself as an IBMer, ensure your profile and related content is consistent with how you wish to present yourself with colleagues and clients.

Don't pick fights, and be the first to correct your own mistakes.

Try to add value. Provide worthwhile information and perspective. IBM's brand is best represented by its people, and what you publish may reflect on IBM's brand.

Don't use IBM logos or trademarks unless approved to do so.

Detailed Discussion

The IBM Business Conduct Guidelines and laws provide the foundation for IBM's policies and guidelines for blogs and social computing.

The same principles and guidelines that apply to IBMers' activities in general, as found in the IBM Business Conduct Guidelines, apply to IBMers' activities online. This includes forms of online publishing and discussion, including blogs, wikis, file-sharing, user-generated video and audio, virtual worlds[1] and social networks.

As outlined in the Business Conduct Guidelines, IBM fully respects the legal rights of our employees in all countries in which we operate. In general, what you do on your own time is your affair. However, activities in or outside of work that affect your IBM job performance, the performance of others, or IBM's business interests are a proper focus for company policy.

IBM supports open dialogue and the exchange of ideas.

IBM regards blogs and other forms of online discourse as primarily a form of communication and relationship among individuals. When the company wishes to communicate publicly as a company—whether to the marketplace or to the general public—it has well established means to do so. Only those officially designated by IBM have the authorization to speak on behalf of the company.

However, IBM believes in dialogue among IBMers and with our partners, clients, members of the many communities in which we participate, and the general public. Such dialogue is inherent in our business model of innovation, and in our commitment to the development of open standards. We believe that IBMers can both derive and provide important benefits from exchanges of perspective.

One of IBMers' core values is "trust and personal responsibility in all relationships." As a company, IBM trusts—and expects—IBMers to exercise personal responsibility whenever they participate in social media. This includes not violating the trust of those with whom they are engaging. IBMers should not use these media for covert marketing or public relations. If and when members of IBM's Communications, Marketing, Sales, or other functions engaged in advocacy for the company have the authorization to participate in social media, they should identify themselves as such.

Know the IBM Business Conduct Guidelines. If you have any confusion about whether you ought to publish something online, chances are the BCGs will resolve it. Pay particular attention to what the BCGs have to say about proprietary information, about avoiding misrepresentation and about competing in the field. If, after checking the BCG's, you are still unclear as to the propriety of a post, it is best to refrain and seek the advice of management.

Be who you are. We believe in transparency and honesty; anonymity is not an option. When discussing topics relevant to IBM, you must use your real name, be clear who you are, and identify that you work for IBM. If you have a vested interest in something you are discussing, be the first to point it out. But also be smart about protecting yourself and your privacy. What you publish will be around for a long time, so consider the content carefully and also be judicious in disclosing personal details.

Be thoughtful about how you present yourself in online social networks. The lines between public and private, personal and professional are blurred in online social networks. By virtue of identifying yourself as an IBMer within a social network, you are now connected to your colleagues, managers and even IBM's clients. You should ensure that content associated with you is consistent with your work at IBM. If you have joined IBM recently, be sure to update your social profiles to reflect IBM's guidelines. You may not use IBM logos or trademarks as a part of your postings, including in your identity on a site, unless you are approved to do so.

Speak in the first person. Use your own voice; bring your own personality to the forefront.

Use a disclaimer. Whenever you publish content to any form of digital media, make it clear that what you say there is representative of your views and opinions and not necessarily the views and opinions of IBM. For instance, in your own blog, the following standard disclaimer should be prominently displayed: "The postings on this site are my own and don't necessarily represent IBM's positions, strategies or opinions." If a site does not afford you enough space to include this full disclaimer, you should use your best judgment to position your comments appropriately.

Managers and executives take note: This standard disclaimer does not by itself exempt IBM managers and executives from a special responsibility when participating in online environments. By virtue of their position, they must consider whether personal thoughts they publish may be misunderstood as expressing IBM positions. And a manager should assume that his or her team will read what is written. Public forums are not the place to communicate IBM policies to IBM employees.

Respect copyright and fair use laws. For IBM's protection and well as your own, it is critical that you show proper respect for the laws governing copyright and fair use of copyrighted material owned by others, including IBM's own copyrights and brands. You should never quote more than short excerpts of someone else's work. And it is good general blogging practice to link to others' work. Keep in mind that laws will be different depending on where you live and work.

Protecting confidential and proprietary information. Social computing blurs many of the traditional boundaries between internal and external communications. Be thoughtful about what you publish—particularly on external platforms. You must make sure you do not disclose or use IBM confidential or proprietary information or that of any other person or company in any online social computing platform. For example, ask permission before posting someone's picture in a social network or publishing in a blog a conversation that was meant to be private.

IBM's business performance and other sensitive subjects. Some topics relating to IBM are sensitive and should never be discussed, even if you're expressing your own opinion and using a disclaimer. For example, you must not comment on, or speculate about, IBM's future business performance (including upcoming quarters or future periods), IBM's business plans, unannounced strategies or prospects (including information about alliances), potential acquisitions or divestitures, similar matters involving IBM's competitors, legal or regulatory matters affecting IBM and other similar subjects that could negatively affect IBM. This applies to anyone including conversations with financial analysts, the press, or other third parties (including friends). If you're unsure of the sensitivity of a particular subject, seek advice from your manager or legal team before talking about it or simply refrain from the conversation. IBM policy is not to comment on rumors in any way. You should merely say, "no comment" to rumors. Do not deny or affirm them (or suggest the same in subtle ways), speculate about them, or propagate them by participating in "what if"-type conversations.

Protect IBM's clients, business partners, and suppliers. Clients, partners, or suppliers should not be cited or obviously referenced without their approval. Externally, never identify a client, partner, or supplier by name without permission and never discuss confidential details of a client engagement. Internal social computing platforms permit suppliers and business partners to participate so be sensitive to who will see your content. If a client hasn't given explicit permission for their name to be used, think carefully about the content you're going to publish on any internal social media and get the appropriate permission where necessary.

It is acceptable to discuss general details about kinds of projects and to use non-identifying pseudonyms for a client (e.g., Client 123) so long as the information provided does not make it easy for someone to identify the client or violate any non-disclosure or intellectual property agreements that may be in place with the client. Be thoughtful about the types of information that you share, which may inadvertently lead others to deduce which clients, partners, and suppliers that you are working with. This might include travel plans or publishing details about your current location or where you are working on a given day. Furthermore, your blog or online social network is not the place to conduct confidential business with a client, partner, or supplier.

Respect your audience and your coworkers. Remember that IBM is a global organization whose employees and clients reflect a diverse set of customs, values, and points of view. Don't be afraid to be yourself, but do so respectfully. This includes not only the obvious (no ethnic slurs, personal insults, obscenity, etc.) but also proper consideration of privacy and of topics that may be considered objectionable or inflammatory—such as politics and religion. For example, if your blog is hosted on an IBM-owned property, avoid these topics and focus on subjects that are business-related. If your blog is self-hosted, use your best judgment and be sure to make it clear that the views and opinions expressed are yours alone and do not represent the official views of IBM. Further, be thoughtful when using tools hosted outside of IBM's protected Intranet environment to communicate among fellow employees about IBM or IBM related matters. Also, while it is fine for IBMers to disagree, please don't use your external blog or other online social media to air your differences in an inappropriate manner.

Add value. IBM's brand is best represented by its people and everything you publish online reflects upon it. Blogs and social networks that are hosted on IBM-owned domains should be used in a way that adds value to IBM's business. If it helps you, your coworkers, our clients, or our partners to do their jobs and solve problems; if it helps to improve knowledge or skills; if it contributes directly or indirectly to the improvement of IBM's products, processes and policies; if it builds a sense of community; or if it helps to promote IBM's Values, then it is adding value. It is best to stay within your sphere of expertise, and whenever you are presenting something as fact, make sure it is a fact. Though not directly business-related, background information you choose to share about yourself, such as information about your family or personal interests, may be useful in helping establish a relationship between you and your readers, but it is entirely your choice whether to share this information.

Don't pick fights. When you see misrepresentations made about IBM by media, analysts, or by other bloggers, you may certainly use your blog—or add comments on the original discussion—to point that out. Always do so with respect, stick to the facts, and identify your appropriate affiliation to IBM. Also, if you speak about a competitor, you must make sure that what you say is factual and that it does not disparage the competitor. Avoid unnecessary or unproductive arguments. Brawls may earn traffic, but nobody wins in the end and you may negatively affect your own, and IBM's, reputation in the process. Don't try to settle scores or goad competitors or others into inflammatory debates. Here and in other areas of public discussion, make sure that what you are saying is factually correct.

Be the first to respond to your own mistakes. If you make an error, be up front about your mistake and correct it quickly, as this can help to restore trust. If you choose to modify content that was previously posted, such as editing a blog post, make it clear that you have done so.

Adopt a warm, open, and approachable tone. Remember that much of IBM's image is developed by the public's interaction with real IBMers. We all want that image to be a positive one. Your tone, your openness, and your approachability can help with that, just as they can with your own personal "brand".

Use your best judgment. Remember that there are always consequences to what you publish. If you're about to publish something that makes you even the slightest bit uncomfortable, review the suggestions above and think about why that is. If you're still unsure, and it is related to IBM business, feel free to discuss it with your manager. Ultimately, however, you have sole responsibility for what you post to your blog or publish in any form of online social media.

Don't forget your day job. You should make sure that your online activities do not interfere with your job or commitments to customers.

Endnotes

[1] Virtual worlds present a number of unique circumstances, not all of which are covered in these guidelines. Please refer to the companion, "Virtual worlds Guidelines" for additional guidelines around identity, behavior, appearance, and intellectual property.

Index

A

A/B testing, 12
access to information for
    influencers, 81-85, 168-169
activities at IBM, 136
advocates, gaining, 77
  continuous feedback, 85-87
  individual perspective, finding via
      search, 78-80
  recognition for influencers, 81-85,
      168-169
  truth in use, 88-91
  via leadership, 78
agility, 3, 7-8
Allen, David, 34
America's Great Outdoors
    (ideation), 38

amplification of social media
    messaging, 48, 55-59,
    114-115
analyst firm (picking fights
    example), 66-67
analyst reports, influence and
    transparency, 14-20
analytics
  Google Alerts, 95-97
  IBM CMO study (2011), 94-95
apologizing publicly, 148-150
Apple
  public apologies, 148-149
  social engagement, 4-5
audience
  respecting, 177
  risks associated with, 146-148
  subset populations, 151-152

authentic voice, limitations
    of, 59
author contact information, 170
availablogging, 115, 126

B

Barger, Christopher, 172
BBS (bulletin board system), 28
BCGs (Business Conduct
    Guidelines), 173-175
Berger, David, 171
Blanchard, Ken, 129
blogging
    at IBM, 134-135
    as outbound social networking
        tool, 104-105
bookmark sharing at IBM, 136
brands, protecting online,
    152-153
bring your own device
    (BYOD), 137
broadcast tweets, 102
bulletin board system (BBS), 28
Business Conduct Guidelines
    (BCGs), 173-175
business partners,
    protecting, 177
Bynkii blog, when to engage in
    online battles, 69-70
BYOD (bring your own
    device), 137

C

Carter, Sandy, 2, 132
CEMEX (ideation), 39
CEOs, participation in social
    media, 143-144

Champions, 82-84
Chrysler, agility, 7
clients, protecting, 177
CMO study (2011), 94-95
Cognos® Consumer Insight, 80
collaboration tools at IBM,
    132-138
comfort level for social product
    managers, 169-170
comment spam, 153
communities at IBM, 135
community input, gaining, 77
    continuous feedback, 85-87
    individual perspective, finding via
        search, 78-80
    recognition for influencers, 81-85,
        168-169
    truth in use, 88-91
    via leadership, 78
community relationship
    development by real-world
    interactions, 116-123
company, promoting online
    in combination with self and
        product, 27-30
    representing the company, 41-44
competition
    picking fights with, reasons for,
        64-65
    as social media audience, 147-148
confidential information,
    protecting, 176
confidentiality, risk of
    breaching, 154-155
Congressional hearings,
    correcting public record,
    71-72

Connections, ideation in, 41
continuous feedback from
    influencers, 85-87
conversations, starting, 51
copyright, 176
corporate blogs, personal blogs
    versus, 105
corporate collaboration
    at IBM, 132-138
    need for, 130-132
coworkers, respecting, 177
crisis management, 7, 53-55
critics, engagement with,
    63-64, 76
    isolating trolls, 73-75
    IT industry analyst example,
        66-67
    Microsoft example, 65-66
    reasons for, 64-65
    risk management via, 67-68
    when to engage, 68-72
cultural change, social policy
    and, 20-22
customer insight, importance of,
    94-95
customer relationship
    development in real-world
        interactions, 122-123
customers, reaching, 87-88

D

Davis, Joyce, 82, 168
"day in the life" of social
    product managers, 158-160
debate. *See* picking fights
defense/offense, 47
    situation analysis, 47-51
    timing, 48, 52-55

unintended consequences, 48,
    59-61
volume and amplification, 48,
    55-59
demographics, audience
    fragmented by, 151-152
Digg, 103
Digital IBMer program, 43
direct feedback loop for social
    product managers, 24-26
disclaimers, 176
Doctor Who (television show), 32
documentation on
    OpenNTF.org, 120
downloads, names for, 56-57
Duff, Tom, 54
DyDeCom, friendships and
    social business, 125

E

earned success, social business
    and, 8
Edwards, Ben, 88
Elgort, Bruce, 119
email, changes in social
    business, 139
emotion, risk of, 148-150
employee profiles at IBM,
    133-134
engagement, 3-6
    with critics. *See* critics,
        engagement with
    with Google Alerts, 96
    via leadership, 78
    with trolls, 74
enterprise social networks (ESNs)
    at IBM, 132-138
    need for, 130-132

F

Facebook, 106-108
  language translation in, 164
fair use, 176
fake Twitter accounts, 153
feedback
  continuous feedback from
    influencers, 85-87
  participation in feedback sites,
    110-111
  for social product managers,
    24-26
fights
  avoiding, 178
  picking, 63-64
    isolating trolls, 73-75
    IT industry analyst example, 66-67
    Microsoft example, 65-66
    reasons for, 64-65
    risk management via, 67-68
    when to engage, 68-72
file sharing at IBM, 133
filenames, changing, 56-57
forums
  Apple, 4-5
  participation in, 110-111
  as social engagement, 5
foursquare, 4, 110, 126
Freeman, Nathan, 70, 119
friendships from real-world
    interactions, 123-127
future of social product
    management, 163
  inclusiveness, 164-165
  organizational alignment,
    163-164
  selectivity, 165
  technology, 165-166

G

Gallagher, Sean, 16
The Gap, crisis management, 7
Generation Open (GenO), 136
Get Bold! (Carter), 2, 132
Getting Things Done (GTD)
    methodology, 34
Gillmor, Dan, 17
globally integrated
    enterprises, 138
Globe Trekker (television
    show), 31
Google A/B testing, 12
Google Alerts, 95-97
Google Apps, 72
Google+, 110
GTD (Getting Things Done)
    methodology, 34
guidelines. *See* IBM Social
    Computing Guidelines

H

Hodge, Jeremy, 25
Hoerle, Amy, 87
Hollingsworth, Tony, 124
HootSuite, 101

I

IBM, social collaboration tools
    at, 132-138
IBM Business Conduct
    Guidelines, 173-175
IBM Champions, 82-84
IBM CMO study (2011), 94-95
IBM Connections app, initial
    release of, 23-24
IBM Design Partners, 81

IBM Greenhouse, 88
IBM Social Computing
  Guidelines
  body, 173-174
  cultural change and, 20-22
  development of, 171-172
  explained, 174-179
  introduction, 172-173
  for picking fights, 65
IBM XWork Server,
  development of, 25
IdeaJam ideation software, 40
ideation
  examples of, 38-39
  explained, 39-41
identity risks, 152-153
inbound social networking
  tools, 95
  Google Alerts, 95-97
  LinkedIn, 97-99
  Quora, 102-103
  Twitter, 99-102
inclusiveness, future of social
  product management,
  164-165
Indiana University BBS system,
  27-28
individual perspective, finding
  via search, 78-80
individual relationship
  development by real-world
  interactions, 121-123
influence, transparency and,
  14-20
influencers, gaining, 77
  continuous feedback, 85-87
  individual perspective, finding via
    search, 78-80

recognition for influencers, 81-85,
  168-169
truth in use, 88-91
via leadership, 78
inside sales, effect of social
  business on, 139-140
installation problems, 36
internal corporate
  communication
  at IBM, 132-138
  need for, 130-132
internal risks, 154-155
iPhone, Lotus Notes capability
  in, 37-38
isolating trolls, 73-75
Issa, Darrel, 71-72
IT industry analyst firm, picking
  fights example, 66-67

J-K-L

jams (online), 38
Jobs, Steve, 148

Kozanecka, Olga, 152

language
  audience fragmented by, 151-152
  translation in Facebook, 164
leadership, gaining
  influencers, 78
Li, Charlene, 131
LinkedIn, 97-99
LinkedIn Answers, 98-99
location-based services for
  real-world interactions,
  126-127
Lotus Notes
  on iPhone, 37-38
  UI design, 85-86

M

Mack, Eric, 34
marketing departments, social
    business' effect on, 22-24
Mayfield, Ross, 16
measuring ROI on social
    business tools, 138-140
meatspace, 113
message amplification by
    real-world interactions,
    114-115
microblogging at IBM, 134-135
Microsoft
    marketing comparison with IBM
        products, 147-148
    picking fights with, 65-66
millennials, defined, 3
Mittleman, Danny, 98
Mooney, Paul, 56-57
MyStarbucksIdea.com
    (ideation), 38

N–O

name checking, 149
narrowing the audience, 146

O'Neil, Brian, 122-123
Obama, Barack, 38, 40
Ochs, Jake, 32
offense/defense, 47
    situation analysis, 47-51
    timing, 48, 52-55
    unintended consequences, 48,
        59-61
    volume and amplification, 48,
        55-59
online communities at IBM, 135

online fights, 63-64
    isolating trolls, 73-75
    IT industry analyst example,
        66-67
    Microsoft example, 65-66
    reasons for, 64-65
    risk management via, 67-68
    when to engage, 68-72
online jams, 38
open source, 118
OpenNTF.org, 119-121
organizational alignment, future
    of social product
    management, 163-164
Orkut, 151
outbound social networking
    tools, 103-104, 110
    blogging, 104-105
    Facebook, 106-108
    SlideShare, 109-110
    Twitter, 105-106

P

pages (Facebook), 107-108
Palmisano, Sam, 16
Perdue Farms, product
    marketing, 12
Periera, Vitor, 125
personal blogs, corporate blogs
    versus, 105
personal branding, 30-34
Peters, Tom, 30
picking fights, 63-64
    isolating trolls, 73-75
    IT industry analyst example,
        66-67
    Microsoft example, 65-66

reasons for, 64-65

risk management via, 67-68

when to engage, 68-72

Pinterest, 103

podcasts, 110

politics in picking fights, 69

positioning product, 35-39

private communication, risk of
publicizing, 154-155

product, promoting online,
35-39

in combination with self and
company, 27-30

product development, effect of
social tools on, 140-143

product managers. *See also* social
product managers

changing role of, 162-163

role of, 11-13

social product managers versus,
13-14

work environment of, 138

professional debate, defined, 69

progressive disclosure, 52

proprietary information,
protecting, 176

public apologies, 148-150

Q-R

Quora, 102-103

Radicati Group, influence and
transparency, 14-20

Radicati, Sara, 17

Raven, Mary Beth, 85-86

reach

of Facebook pages, 107-108

of social media messaging, 55-59

reaching wrong audience,
146-148

real-world interactions, 113-114

community relationship
development, 116-123

friendship development, 123-127

message amplification, 114-115

recognition, providing for
influencers, 81-85, 168-169

Reddit, 103

reference stories, 89-91

relationship development by
real-world interactions,
116-123

representing the company, 41-44

researching social networking
tools, 167-168

return on investment (ROI)
for social business tools,
138-140

risk management, 145

identity risks, 152-153

internal risks, 154-155

in picking fights, 67-68

public apologies, 148-150

reaching wrong audience,
146-148

subset populations, 151-152

ROI (return on investment)
for social business tools,
138-140

Rometty, Ginni, 43

rumors, responding to, 53-55

S

sales, effect of social business on, 139-140

sales departments, effect of social business on, 22-24

Sampson, Michael, 15, 18-19

Schick, Jeff, 59-60

SCORE program, 7

searches, finding individual perspectives via, 78-80

selectivity, future of social product management, 165

self, promoting online
in combination with product and company, 27-30
personal branding, 30-34

sensitive topics, avoiding in social media, 176

Shapiro, Justine, 31

Share, Jacob, 75

sharing at IBM
bookmarks, 136
files, 133

Shift (ideation), 39

situation analysis, 47-51

SlideShare, 109-110

SmallBlue, 139

smartphones at IBM, 137

social business
agility, 3, 7-9
benefits of, 160-161
characteristics of, 3-4
defined, 1
earned success and, 8
effect on product development, 140-143

engagement, 3-6
explained, 1-3
at IBM, 132-138
need for, 130-132
return on investment (ROI), 138-140
sales and marketing departments, effect on, 22-24
tactical analysis, 47
situation analysis, 47-51
timing, 48, 52-55
unintended consequences, 48, 59-61
volume and amplification, 48, 55-59
transparency, 3, 6-7
who should participate, 143-144

Social Computing Guidelines (at IBM)
body, 173-174
cultural change and, 20-22
development of, 171-172
explained, 174-179
introduction, 172-173
for picking fights, 65

social computing policies, creating, 166-167

social media
what to post, 48-51
when to post, 52-55

social networking, 1

social networking tools
forums and feedback sites, 110-111
future of social product management, 165-166

inbound tools, 95
  Google Alerts, 95-97
  LinkedIn, 97-99
  Quora, 102-103
  Twitter, 99-102
outbound tools, 103-104, 110
  blogging, 104-105
  Facebook, 106-108
  SlideShare, 109-110
  Twitter, 105-106
researching, 167-168
social policy, cultural change
  and, 20-22
social product managers. *See also*
  product managers
changing role of, 162-163
comfort level of, 169-170
"day in the life," 158-160
direct feedback loop, 24-26
duties of, 161-162
effect of social tools on, 140-143
forums and feedback sites,
  110-111
future of, 163
  inclusiveness, 164-165
  organizational alignment, 163-164
  selectivity, 165
  technology, 165-166
gaining influencers
  continuous feedback, 85-87
  individual perspective, finding via
    search, 78-80
  recognition for influencers, 81-85,
    168-169
  truth in use, 88-91
  via leadership, 78

inbound social networking
  tools, 95
  Google Alerts, 95-97
  LinkedIn, 97-99
  Quora, 102-103
  Twitter, 99-102
influence and transparency, 14-20
opportunities for, 162
outbound social networking tools,
  103-104, 110
  blogging, 104-105
  Facebook, 106-108
  SlideShare, 109-110
  Twitter, 105-106
product managers versus, 13-14
real-world interactions, 113-114
  community relationship development,
    116-123
  friendship development, 123-127
  message amplification, 114-115
self, product, company promotion
  combination of, 27-30
  company representation, 41-45
  ideation, 39-41
  personal branding, 30-34
  product positioning, 35-39
  in social policy, 20-22
  as unique voice, 35
software development, XPages
  Extension Library, 119-120
solution selling, 89-91
Sorentino, Frank, 143
spam, as identity risk, 153
Starbucks (ideation), 38, 40
starting conversations, 51
subset populations, 151-152

suppliers, protecting, 177
support forums
  Apple, 4-5
  participation in, 110-111
  as social engagement, 5

T

tablets at IBM, 137
tactical analysis, 47
  situation analysis, 47-51
  timing, 48, 52-55
  unintended consequences, 48,
    59-61
  volume and amplification, 48,
    55-59
technology, future of social
    product management,
    165-166
Tencent QQ, 151
The Gap, crisis management, 7
Tillmans, Christian, 50
time management, 34
  in social business, 121
timing in social product
    management, 48, 52-55
tools
  forums and feedback sites,
    110-112
  future of social product
    management, 165-166
  inbound social networking
    tools, 95
  Google Alerts, 95-97
  LinkedIn, 97-99
  Quora, 102-103
  Twitter, 99-102

outbound social networking tools,
    103-104, 110
  blogging, 104-105
  Facebook, 106-108
  SlideShare, 109-110
  Twitter, 105-106
  researching, 167-168
translation in Facebook, 164
transparency, 3, 6-7
  influence and, 14-20
trend analysis tool, Twitter
    as, 101
trending topics in Twitter, 164
Tripcony, Tim, 43
TripIt, 126
trolls, isolating, 73-75
truth in use, 88-91
"try before you buy" policies,
    88-91
Twitter
  fake accounts, 153
  as inbound source, 99-102
  as outbound social networking
    tool, 105-106
  trending topics, 164

U-V

UI design, continuous feedback
    in, 85-86
Unilever, subset populations of
    audience, 152
unintended consequences, 48,
    59-61
unique voice, 35
  developing, 169-170
  in leadership, 78

user groups, community
    relationship development
    by real-world interactions,
    116-123

validation of trolls, 74
value, adding in social
    media, 178
virtual worlds, 179
volume of social media
    messaging, 48, 55-59

W–X–Y–Z

Watson, 166
We the Media (Gillmor), 17
Welch, John, 69
wikis
 defined, 20
 at IBM, 135
Withers, Paul, 119

Xing, 103
XPages Extension Library
    software development,
    119-120
XWork Server, development
    of, 25

YouTube, 110

Zingale, Tony, 59-60

ED BRILL

OPTING IN

LESSONS IN SOCIAL BUSINESS FROM
A FORTUNE 500 PRODUCT MANAGER

Safari
Books Online

FREE
Online Edition

Your purchase of *Opting In* includes access to a free online edition for 45 days through the **Safari Books Online** subscription service. Nearly every IBM Press book is available online through **Safari Books Online**, along with thousands of books and videos from publishers su as Addison-Wesley Professional, Cisco Press, Exam Cram, O'Reilly Media, Prentice Hall, Que and Sams.

Safari Books Online is a digital library providing searchable, on-demand access to thousand of technology, digital media, and professional development books and videos from leading publishers. With one monthly or yearly subscription price, you get unlimited access to learnir tools and information on topics including mobile app and software development, tips and tric on using your favorite gadgets, networking, project management, graphic design, and much more.

 Addison Wesley Adobe Press ALPHA Cisco Press FT Press IBM Press Microsoft Press New Riders O'REILLY

 Peachpit Press PRENTICE HALL QUE Redbooks SAMS SAS Publishing vmware PRESS WILEY WROX